Charles Baudelaire

Charles Baudelaire

A Lyric Poet in the Era of High Capitalism

---◆---

WALTER BENJAMIN

Translated by Harry Zohn

VERSO

London • New York

This edition first published by Verso 2023
First published by New Left Books 1973
© Verso 2023

'The Paris of the Second Empire in Baudelaire' and 'Some Motifs in Baudelaire'
first published in one volume as Charles Baudelaire, *Ein Lyriker im Zeitalter des
Hochkapitalismus*, edited by Rolf Tiedemann © Suhrkamp Verlag 1969; addendum
to 'The Paris of the Second Empire in Baudelaire' first published in *Das Paris
des Second Empire bei Baudelaire* © Suhrkamp Verlag 1971; this translation of
'Some Motifs in Baudelaire' first published in *Illuminations*, edited by Hannah
Arendt © Harcourt Brace Jovanovich and Jonathan Cape 1968, 1970; 'Paris
– the Capital of the Nineteenth Century' first published in Walter Benjamin,
Schriften, 2 vols © Suhrkamp Verlag,1955; this (slightly emended) translation
of 'Paris – the Capital of the Nineteenth Century' by Quintin Hoare, first
published in *New Left Review*, no. 48, 1968, translation © *New Left Review*, 1968.

Verso
UK: 6 Meard Street, London W1F 0EG
US: 388 Atlantic Avenue, Brooklyn, NY 11217
versobooks.com

Verso is the imprint of New Left Books

ISBN-13: 978-1-80429-045-3
ISBN-13: 978-1-80429-102-3 (US EBK)
ISBN-13: 978-1-80429-101-6 (UK EBK)

British Library Cataloguing in Publication Data
A catalogue record for this book is available from the British Library

Library of Congress Cataloging-in-Publication Data
A catalog record for this book is available from the Library of Congress

Printed and Bound by CPI Group (UK) Ltd, Croydon, CR0 4YY

Bibliographical note to the English edition

The three texts in this volume consist of three different stages of Walter Benjamin's uncompleted Paris Arcades project (*Passagenarbeit*), the cultural study of nineteenth-century Paris on which he worked with increasing intensity from the late twenties until his death in 1940.

'The Paris of the Second Empire in Baudelaire' was completed in 1938, at a time when Benjamin planned to make a separate book out of the material for the project which he had collected on Baudelaire. It was conceived as the central section of three which were to constitute the Baudelaire book. The other two sections exist only as fragments in German – 'Baudelaire as Allegorist' and 'The Commodity as a Subject of Poetry'. Of the three parts of 'The Paris of the Second Empire in Baudelaire', 'The *Bohème*' was first published in *Charles Baudelaire – Ein Lyriker im Zeitalter des Hochkapitalismus* (Frankfurt, 1969), 'The *Flâneur*' in *Neue Rundschau*, vol. 4, 1967, and 'Modernism' in *Das Argument*, no. 46, 1968. The Addendum was first published in *Das Paris des Second Empire bei Baudelaire* (Berlin and Weimar, 1971). This (East German) edition, based on the original handwritten manuscript in the Benjamin Archive in Potsdam, differs textually in only a few respects from the Frankfurt 1969 edition, based on the typescript in the Frankfurt Archive; it does however contain Benjamin's uncompleted methodological introduction, omitted from the Frankfurt edition, and it is this that is printed here as an Addendum. (For indications of the other differences between the manuscript and the typescript versions, see Rosemarie Heise's introduction to the Berlin/Weimar edition.)

'Some Motifs in Baudelaire' was completed in 1939, written as a result of a critique by T. W. Adorno of 'The Paris of the Second Empire in Baudelaire', whose central part it was intended to replace. It was first published in the *Zeitschrift für Sozialforschung*, vol. 8, 1939.

'Paris – the Capital of the Nineteenth Century' was completed in 1935 as an exposé or draft of the project as a whole. It was first published in Walter Benjamin, *Schriften*, 2 vols (Frankfurt, 1955).

Translator's note: Benjamin's own references have been retained throughout, except for those to Baudelaire's translations of Edgar Allan Poe (Baudelaire, *Oeuvres complètes*, vol. 10, Paris, 1937), where this English edition uses Poe's original text.

Some quotations from French sources have been translated from Benjamin's German text. All quotations from Baudelaire have been translated from the original French. Poems from *Les Fleurs du mal* are quoted in the English translation, by various hands, published by New Directions (*The Flowers of Evil*, New York, 1955). Other verse translation is by me. I am grateful to my colleague at Brandeis University, Murray Sachs, for checking the French translation.

I have taken this opportunity to make minor emendations to the translation of 'Some Motifs in Baudelaire', originally published as 'On Some Motifs in Baudelaire'.

H.Z.

Acknowledgement: We wish to thank New Directions Publishing Corporation for their kind permission to use extracts from Charles Baudelaire's *The Flowers of Evil*, edited by Jackson and Marthiel Mathews; and the University of California Press for permission to use C. F. MacIntyre's translation, 'To a Passer-by'.

The Paris of the
Second Empire in Baudelaire

Une capitale n'est pas absolument nécessaire à l'homme

('A capital is not absolutely necessary for man.')

– Senancour

I. The *Bohème**

The *bohème* appears in a revealing context in the writings of Marx. In it he includes the professional conspirators with whom he concerns himself in his detailed note on the memoirs of the police agent, de la Hodde, which appeared in the *Neue Rheinische Zeitung* in 1850. To bring to mind the physiognomy of Baudelaire means to speak of the resemblance which he displays with this political type. Marx outlines this type as follows: 'The development of proletarian conspiracies produced a need for a division of labour. Their members were divided into occasional conspirators, *conspirateurs d'occasion*, i.e. workers who carried on conspiracies only in addition to

* [At the beginning of this manuscript there are two sheets with the following notations. '*Sheet 1:* A section of approximately nine pages is missing here. It presents the connection between the increasing standardization of Paris architecture, Haussmann's work, and the Bonapartist depotism. It characterizes the attempts of the *feuilleton* to create, by means of its phantasmagoria, a diversion in the tedium of urban life. *Sheet 2:* A section of approximately six pages is missing here. It gives a brief history of the various generations of the *bohème*. It characterizes the *bohème dorée* of Gautier and Nerval; the *bohème* of the generation of Baudelaire, Asselineau, Delvau; and, finally, the latest proletarianized *bohème* whose spokesman was Jules Vallès. There follows the complete text to the end.' *Editorial note in the German edition.*]

their other employment, who only attended the meetings and kept themselves in readiness to appear at the assembly point upon orders from the leader, and into professional conspirators who devoted their entire activity to the conspiracy and made a living from it. . . . The social position of this class predetermined its whole character. . . . Their uncertain existence, which in specific cases depended more on chance than on their activities, their irregular life whose only fixed stations were the taverns of the wine dealers – the gathering places of the conspirators – and their inevitable acquaintanceship with all sorts of dubious people place them in that sphere of life which in Paris is called *la bohème*.'[1]

In passing it should be noted that Napoleon III himself began his rise in a milieu that is related to the one described above. As we know, one of the tools of his presidential period was the Society of the Tenth of December whose cadres, according to Marx, had been supplied by 'the whole indeterminate, disintegrated, fluctuating mass which the French call *la bohème*'.[2] During his emperorship Napoleon continued his conspiratory customs. Surprising proclamations and mystery-mongering, sudden sallies, and impenetrable irony were part of the *raison d'état* of the Second Empire. The same traits may be found in Baudelaire's theoretical writings. He usually presents his views apodictically. Discussion is not his style; he avoids it even when the glaring contradictions in the theses which he gradually appropriates require discussion. He dedicated his 'Salon de 1846' to 'the bourgeois'; he appears as their advocate, and his manner is not that of an *advocatus diaboli*. Later, for example in his invectives against the school of *bon sens*, he attacks the '"*honnête bourgeoise* and the notary, the person such a woman holds in

1. Karl Marx and Friedrich Engels, review of Chenu, *Les conspirateurs*, Paris, 1850, and Lucien de la Hodde, *La naissance de la République en février 1848*, Paris, 1850; quoted from *Die Neue Zeit*, 4 (1886), p. 555. Proudhon, who wanted to dissociate himself from the professional conspirators, occasionally called himself a 'new man – a man whose style is not the barricades but discussion, a man who could sit at a table with the chief of police every evening and could take all the de la Hoddes of the world into his confidence' (quoted in Gustave Geffroy, *L'enfermé*, Paris, 1897, pp. 180ff.).

2. Marx, *Der achtzehnte Brumaire des Louis Bonaparte*, edited by David Riazanov, Vienna, 1917, p. 73.

respect, in the manner of the most rabid *bohémien*.[3] Around 1850 he proclaimed that art could not be separated from utility; a few years thereafter he championed *l'art pour l'art*. In all this he was no more concerned with preparing his public for this than Napoleon III was when he switched, almost overnight and behind the French parliament's back, from protective tariffs to free trade. These traits, at any rate, make it understandable that official criticism, above all Jules Lemaître, perceived very little of the theoretical energy contained in Baudelaire's prose.

Marx continued in his description of the *conspirateurs de profession* as follows: 'The only condition for revolution is for them the adequate organization of their conspiracy. . . . They embrace inventions which are supposed to perform revolutionary miracles: fire bombs, destructive machines with magical effects, riots which are to be the more miraculous and surprising the less rational their foundation is. Occupying themselves with such projects, they have no other aim but the immediate one of overthrowing the existing government, and they profoundly despise the more theoretical enlightenment of the workers as to their class interests. Hence their anger – not proletarian but plebeian – at the *habits noirs* (black coats), the more or less educated people who represent that side of the movement and of whom they can never become entirely independent, since these are the official representatives of the party.'[4] Baudelaire's political insights do not go fundamentally beyond those of the professional conspirators. Whether he bestows his sympathies upon clerical reaction or upon the revolution of 1848, their expression remains abrupt and their foundation fragile. The image he presented in the February days – brandishing a rifle on some Paris street corner and shouting 'Down with General Aupick!' (his own stepfather) – is a case in point. He could, in any case, have adopted Flaubert's statement, 'Of all of politics I understand only one thing: the revolt.' It could then have been understood in the sense of the final passage in a note which has come down to us

3. Charles Baudelaire, *Oeuvres*, edited by Yves-Gérard Le Dantec, 2 vols, Paris, 1931–2 [Bibliothèque de la Pléïade, nos 1 and 7], vol. II, p. 415 (henceforth cited only by volume and page number).

4. Marx and Engels, review of Chenu and de la Hodde, op. cit., p. 556.

together with his sketches on Belgium: 'I say *"Long live the revolution!"* as I would say *"Long live destruction! Long live penance! Long live chastisement! Long live death!"* I would be happy not only as a victim; it would not displease me to play the hangman as well – so as to feel the revolution from both sides! All of us have the republican spirit in our blood as we have syphilis in our bones; we have a democratic and a syphilitic infection.'[5]

What Baudelaire expresses thus could be called the metaphysics of the *provocateur*. In Belgium, where he wrote this note, he was for a while regarded as a French police spy. Actually, such arrangements were hardly considered strange, and on 20 December 1854 Baudelaire wrote to his mother with reference to the literary stipendiaries of the police: 'My name will never appear in their shameful registers.'[6] What gained Baudelaire such a reputation in Belgium can hardly have been only the hostility which he displayed toward Hugo, who was proscribed in France but acclaimed in Belgium. His devastating irony contributed to the origin of that rumour; it may have given him pleasure to spread it himself. The seeds of the *culte de la blague*, which reappears in Georges Sorel and has become an integral part of Fascist propaganda, are first found in Baudelaire. The spirit in which Céline wrote his *Bagatelles pour un massacre*, and its very title, go back directly to a diary entry by Baudelaire: 'A fine conspiracy could be organized for the purpose of exterminating the Jewish race.'[7] The Blanquist Rigault, who ended his conspiratory career as police chief of the Paris Commune, seems to have had the same macabre humour, frequently mentioned in documents about Baudelaire. In Charles Prolès's *Hommes de la révolution de 1871* we read that 'Rigault, despite his great coldbloodedness, was invariably a wild wag. That was an integral part of him, down to his fanaticism.'[8] Even the terroristic pipe-dream which Marx encountered among the *conspirateurs* has its counterpart in Baudelaire. 'If I ever regain the vigour and energy which I had on a few occasions,' he wrote to his mother on 23 December 1865, 'I will vent my anger in terrifying books. I want to raise the whole human race against me.

5. II, 728.   6. Baudelaire, *Lettres à sa mère*, Paris, 1932, p. 83.
7. II, 666.

8. Charles Prolès, *Les hommes de la révolution de 1871. Raoul Rigault.* Paris, 1898, p. 9.

The delight this would give me would console me for everything.'[9]
This suppressed rage – *la rogne* – was the emotion which a half
century of barricade fights had nurtured in Parisian professional
conspirators.

'It is they,' writes Marx about these conspirators, 'who erect the
first barricades and command them.'[10] The barricade was, indeed,
at the centre of the conspirative movement. It had revolutionary
tradition on its side. Over four thousand barricades had studded
the city during the July Revolution.[11] When Fourier looked for an
example of *travail non salarié mais passionné*, he found none that
was more obvious than the building of barricades. In his *Les
Misérables* Hugo has given an impressive picture of those barricades, while disregarding the people who manned them. 'Everywhere an invisible police of the revolt was on guard. It maintained
order – that is, the night. . . . Eyes that might have looked down on
these towering shadows from above might have encountered here
and there an indistinct glow that revealed broken, irregular outlines, profiles of strange constructions. In these ruins something
resembling lights moved. In these places stood the barricades.'[12] In
the fragmentary 'Address to Paris' which was to have concluded the
Fleurs du mal, Baudelaire does not say farewell to the city without
invoking its barricades; he remembers its 'magic cobblestones which
rise up to form fortresses'.[13] These stones, to be sure, are 'magic'
because Baudelaire's poem says nothing about the hands which set
them in motion. But this very pathos is probably indebted to
Blanquism, for the Blanquist Tridon cries out in a similar vein:
'O force, queen of the barricades, you who shine in the lightning
and in the riot . . . it is toward you that the prisoners stretch their
shackled hands' (*'O force, reine des barricades, toi qui brille dans
l'éclair et dans l'émeute . . . c'est vers toi que les prisonniers tendent
leurs mains enchaînées'*).[14] At the end of the Commune the proletariat

9. Baudelaire, *Lettres à sa mère*, op. cit., p. 278.

10. Marx and Engels, review of Chenu and de la Hodde, op. cit., p. 556.

11. Cf. Ajasson de Grandsagne and Maurice Plaut, *Révolution de 1830. Plan
des combats de Paris aux 27, 28 et 29 juillet*. Paris, n.d.

12. Victor Hugo, *Oeuvres complètes. Edition définitive. Roman VIII: Les
Misérables*, Paris, 1881, pp. 522ff.   13. I, 229.

14. Quoted in Charles Benoist, 'Le "mythe" de la classe ouvrière', in *Revue
des deux mondes*, 1 March 1914, p. 105.

groped its way behind the barricades, as a mortally injured animal withdraws to its lair. The fact that the workers, who had been trained in barricade fighting, did not favour the open battle which was bound to block Thiers's path was partly to blame for the defeat. As a recent historian of the Commune writes, these workers 'preferred battle in their own quarters to an encounter in the open field ... and if it had to be, they preferred to die behind a barricade built of cobblestones from a Paris street'.[15]

In those days Blanqui, the most important of the Paris barricade chiefs, sat in his last prison, the Fort du Taureau. In him and his associates Marx saw, in his review of the June Revolution, 'the true leaders of the proletarian party'.[16] It is hardly possible to over-estimate the revolutionary prestige which Blanqui possessed at that time and preserved up to his death. Before Lenin there was no one else with a clearer profile in the proletariat. His features were engraved in Baudelaire's mind. There is a sheet by him which bears a likeness of Blanqui's head in addition to other improvised drawings.

The concepts which Marx uses in his depiction of the conspiratory milieu in Paris clearly bring out Blanqui's ambivalent position in it. There are good reasons for the traditional view of Blanqui as a putschist. In this view he constitutes the type of politician who, as Marx put it, regards it as his task 'to anticipate the revolutionary developmental process, to bring it artificially to a head, and improvise a revolution without the conditions for one'.[17] If, on the other hand, one opposes to this view existing descriptions of Blanqui, he seems to resemble one of the *habits noirs* who were the disliked competitors of those professional conspirators. An eye-witness has given the following description of Blanqui's Club des Halles: 'If one wishes to get an accurate idea of the impression which one gained from the first moment of Blanqui's revolutionary club in comparison with the two clubs which the Party of Order then had, one should imagine the audience of the Comédie Française on a day on which Racine and Corneille are played, beside the crowd that fills a circus in which acrobats are performing breakneck feats. One was,

15. Georges Laronze, *Histoire de la Commune de 1871*, Paris, 1928, p. 532.
16. Marx, *Der achtzehnte Brumaire des Louis Bonaparte*, op. cit., p. 28.
17. Marx and Engels, review of Chenu and de la Hodde, op. cit., p. 556.

as it were, in a chapel which was devoted to the orthodox rites of conspiracy. The doors were open to all, but only the initiates came back. After a wearisome procession of the suppressed . . . the priest of this place arose. His pretext was that he was going to give a résumé of the complaints of his clients, of the people represented by the half dozen presumptuous and irritated blockheads who had just been heard from. In reality he gave an analysis of the situation. His outward appearance was distinguished, his clothes were immaculate. He had a finely formed head, and his facial expression was calm. Only the wild flashing of his eyes sometimes portended trouble; his eyes were narrow, small, and penetrating, and usually they looked kind rather than hard. His speech was measured, fatherly, and distinct – next to the oratorical style of Thiers, the least declamatory I have heard.'[18] In this account Blanqui appears as a doctrinaire. The *signalement* (description) of the *habit noir* applies down to small details. It was well known that 'the old man' was in the habit of wearing black gloves while lecturing.[19] But the measured seriousness and the impenetrability which were part of Blanqui's make-up appear different in the light in which a statement by Marx places them. 'They are,' so he writes about these professional conspirators, 'the alchemists of the revolution and fully share the disintegration of ideas, the narrow-mindedness, and the obsessions of the earlier alchemists.'[20] This almost automatically results in Baudelaire's image: the enigmatic stuff of allegory in one, the mystery-mongering of the conspirator in the other.

As is to be expected, Marx makes deprecatory remarks about the taverns in which the low conspirators felt at home. The vapour which settled there was familiar to Baudelaire. In it there developed the great poem that is entitled 'Le Vin des chiffoniers' ('The Ragpickers' Wine'); its origin may be placed in the middle of the century. At that time motifs which appear in this poem were being publicly discussed. One thing under discussion was the tax on wine.

18. Report by J.-J. Weiss, quoted in Gustave Geffroy, *L'enfermé*, Paris, 1897, pp. 346ff.

19. Baudelaire appreciated such details. 'Why,' he wrote, 'don't the poor put on gloves when they go begging? They would make a fortune' (II, 424). He attributes this statement to an unnamed person, but it bears the stamp of Baudelaire.

20. Marx and Engels, review of Chenu and de la Hodde, op. cit., p. 556.

The Constituent Assembly of the Republic had promised its repeal, the same promise that had been made in 1830. In his *Class Struggles in France* Marx showed how in the repeal of this tax a demand by the urban proletariat coincided with a demand by the peasants. The tax was equally high on wine for daily consumption and on the finest wines, and it decreased consumption 'by setting up *octrois* (toll houses) at the gates of all cities with over 4,000 inhabitants and changing every town into a foreign country with protective tariffs against French wine'[21]. 'Through the wine tax,' wrote Marx, 'the peasants tested the bouquet of the government.' But this tax also harmed the city-dwellers and forced them to go to taverns outside the city limits in their search for cheap wine. There the tax-free wine which was called the *vin de la barrière* was dispensed. If one can believe H.-A. Frégier, section head at police headquarters, a worker displayed his enjoyment of that wine full of pride and defiance as the only enjoyment granted him. 'There are women who do not hesitate to follow their husbands to the *barrière* (town gate) with their children, who are old enough to work. . . . Afterwards they start their way home half-drunk and act more drunk than they are, so that everyone may notice that they have drunk quite a bit. Sometimes the children follow their parents' example.'[22] 'One thing is certain,' wrote a contemporary observer. 'The wine of the *barrières* has saved the governmental structure from quite a few thrusts.'[23] The wine opened to the disinherited dreams of future revenge and glory. Thus in 'The Ragpickers' Wine':

> On voit un chiffonier qui vient, hochant la tête,
> Buttant, et se cognant aux murs comme un poète,
> Et, sans prendre souci des mouchards, ses sujets,
> Epanche tout son coeur en glorieux projets.
>
> Il prête des serments, dicte des lois sublimes,
> Terrasse les méchants, relève les victimes,

21. Marx, *Die Klassenkämpfe in Frankreich 1848 bis 1850*, Berlin, 1895, p. 87.

22. H.-A. Frégier, *Des classes dangereuses de la population dans les grandes villes et des moyens de les rendre meilleures*, Paris, 1840, vol. 1, p. 86.

23. Edouard Foucaud, *Paris inventeur. Physiologie de l'industrie française*, Paris, 1844, p. 10.

Et sous le firmament comme un dais suspendu
S'enivre des splendeurs de sa propre vertu.[24]

(One sees a ragpicker knocking against the walls
Paying no heed to the spies of the cops, his thralls,
But stumbling like a poet lost in his dreams;
He pours his heart out in stupendous schemes.

He takes great oaths and dictates sublime laws,
Casts down the wicked, aids the victims' cause;
Beneath the sky, like a vast canopy,
He is drunken of his splendid qualities.)

translated by C. F. MacIntyre

When the new industrial processes had given refuse a certain value, ragpickers appeared in the cities in larger numbers. They worked for middlemen and constituted a sort of cottage industry located in the streets. The ragpicker fascinated his epoch. The eyes of the first investigators of pauperism were fixed on him with the mute question as to where the limit of human misery lay. In his book *Des classes dangereuses de la population*, Frégier devotes six pages to the ragpicker. Le Play gives the budget of a Paris ragpicker and his family for the period between 1849 and 1850, presumably the time when Baudelaire's poem was written.[25]

24. I, 120.
25. This budget is a social document not only because of its investigation of a particular family but also because it attempts to make abject misery appear less objectionable by neatly arranging it under rubrics. With the intent of leaving none of its inhumanities undocumented by the laws whose observance it indicates, the totalitarian states have produced the flowering of a seed which, as one may surmise, was already present in an earlier stage of capitalism. The fourth section of this budget of a ragpicker – cultural needs, entertainment, and hygiene – looks as follows: 'Education of the children: The tuition is paid by the employer, 48 francs; book purchases, 1.45 fr. Charitable contributions (workers of this class usually make none). Feasts and holidays – meals taken by the entire family at one of the *barrières* of Paris (8 excursions a year): wine, bread, and roast potatoes, 8 fr. Meals consisting of macaroni prepared with butter and cheese, plus wine on Christmas Day, Shrove Tuesday, Easter and Whitsun: these expenses are given in the first section. Chewing tobacco for the husband (cigar stubs collected by the workingman himself), representing 5 to 34 fr. Snuff for the wife (bought), 18.66 fr. Toys and other presents for the child, 1 fr. Correspondence with relatives: Letters from the

A ragpicker cannot, of course, be part of the *bohème*. But from the littérateur to the professional conspirator, everyone who belonged to the *bohème* could recognize a bit of himself in the ragpicker. Each person was in a more or less obscure state of revolt against society and faced a more or less precarious future. At the proper time he was able to feel with those who were shaking the foundations of this society. The ragpicker was not alone in his dream. He was accompanied by comrades; they, too, were enveloped in the smell of barrels, and they, too, had turned grey in battles. His moustache drooped like an old flag. On his rounds he encountered the *mouchards*, the police informers whom he dominated in his dreams.[26]

---

workingman's brothers who live in Italy, one per year on the average . . .'. 'Addendum. The family's most important resource in case of accident is private charity . . .'. 'Annual savings (the worker makes no provision whatever; he is primarily concerned with giving his wife and his little daughter all the comforts that are compatible with their situation; he makes no savings, but spends every day whatever he earns)' (Frédéric Le Play, *Les ouvriers européens*, Paris, 1855, 274ff.). A sarcastic remark by Buret serves to illustrate the spirit of such an investigation: 'Since humaneness, even plain decency, forbids one to let human beings die like animals, one cannot deny them the charity of a coffin' (Eugène Buret, *De la misère des classes laborieuses en Angleterre et en France*, Paris, 1840, vol. I, p. 266).

26. It is fascinating to observe how the rebellion gradually comes to the fore in the various versions of the poem's concluding stanzas. In the first version these read as follows:

> C'est ainsi que le vin règne par ses bienfaits,
> Et chante ses exploits par le gosier de l'homme.
> Grandeur de la bonté de Celui que tout nomme,
> Qui nous avait déjà donné le doux Sommeil,
> Et voulut ajouter le Vin, fils du Soleil,
> Pour réchauffer le coeur et calmer la souffrance
> De tous les malheureux qui meurent en silence. (I, 605.)

(Thus the wine reigns by virtue of its benefits and sings of its exploits through the throats of men. How great is the kindness of Him whom all things name, who had already given us sweet sleep and who wished to add wine, the son of the sun, to warm the heart and alleviate the suffering of all who die in silence.)

The 1852 version reads as follows:

> Pour apaiser le coeur et calmer la souffrance
> De tous ces innocents qui meurent en silence,
> Dieu leur avait déjà donné le doux sommeil;
> Il ajouta le vin, fils sacré du Soleil. (I, 606.)

Social motifs from everyday life in Paris may already be found in Sainte-Beuve. There they had been captured by lyric poetry, but were not necessarily understood. Penury and alcohol combined in the mind of the cultured man of leisure in a way that differed substantially from the combination in the mind of a Baudelaire.

> Dans ce cabriolet de classe j'examine
> L'homme qui me conduit, qui n'est plus que machine,
> Hideux, à barbe épaisse, à longs cheveux collés;
> Vice, et vin, et sommeil chargent ses yeux sôulés.
>
> Comment l'homme peut-il ainsi tomber? pensais-je,
> Et je me reculais à l'autre coin du siège.[27]

> (In this fine cab I examine the man who is driving me, no more than a machine, hideous, with a thick beard and long, sticky hair. Vice, wine, and sleep make his drunken eyes heavy. How can man deteriorate that way? So I thought, and I drew back to the other corner of the seat.)

This is the beginning of the poem; what follows is an edifying interpretation. Sainte-Beuve asks himself whether his soul is not almost as neglected as the soul of his coachman.

> (To ease the heart and alleviate the suffering of all the innocent people who die in silence, God has already given them sweet sleep; he added wine, sacred son of the sun.)

The final version of 1857 shows a radical change of meaning and reads as follows:

> Pour noyer la rancoeur et bercer l'indolence
> De tous ces vieux maudits qui meurent en silence,
> Dieu, touché de remords, avait fait le sommeil;
> L'Homme ajouta le Vin, fils sacré du Soleil!   (I, 121.)

> (To lull these wretches' sloth and drown the hate
> Of all who mutely die, compassionate,
> God has created sleep's oblivion;
> Man added Wine, divine child of the Sun.)

translated by C. F. MacIntyre

It may be clearly observed how the stanza receives its definite form only as the substance becomes blasphemous.

27. Charles-Augustin Sainte-Beuve, *Les consolations. Pensées d'août*. Paris, 1863, p. 193.

The litany entitled 'Abel et Cain' shows the foundation of the freer and more reasonable view which Baudelaire had of the disinherited. It turns the contest between the biblical brothers into one between eternally irreconcilable races.

> Race d'Abel, dors, bois et mange;
> Dieu te sourit complaisamment.
>
> Race de Cain, dans la fange
> Rampe et meurs misérablement.[28]
>
> (Race of Abel, sleep and drink;
> God smiles on you approvingly.
>
> Race of Cain, in filth and stink
> Grovel and die, miserably.)

translated by Kenneth O. Hanson

The poem consists of sixteen distichs whose beginning is the same in every other one. Cain, the ancestor of the disinherited, appears as the founder of a race, and this race can be none other than the proletariat. In 1838 Granier de Cassagnac published his *Histoire des classes ouvrières et des classes bourgeoises*. This work claimed to give the origin of the proletarians; they form a class of subhumans which has come into being by crossing robbers with prostitutes. Did Baudelaire know these speculations? It is easily possible. What is certain is that Marx, who hailed Granier de Cassagnac as 'the thinker' of Bonapartist reaction, had encountered them. *Capital* parried this racial theory by developing the concept of a 'race of peculiar commodity-owners',[29] by which was meant the proletariat. In precisely this sense does the race which derives from Cain appear in Baudelaire, although he would not have been able to define it. It is the race of those who possess no commodity but their labour-power.

Baudelaire's poem is part of the cycle entitled *Révolte*.[30] Its three

28. I, 136.

29. Marx, *Das Kapital*, edited by Karl Korsch, Berlin, 1932, p. 173 [English edition, *Capital*, vol. 1, London, 1967, p. 172].

30. The title is followed by a prefatory note which was suppressed in the later editions. This note claims that the poems of the group are a very literary reproduction of 'the sophisms of ignorance and anger'. In truth it is not a

components are blasphemous in tone. Baudelaire's Satanism must not be taken too seriously. If it has some significance, it is as the only attitude in which Baudelaire was able to sustain a non-conformist position for any length of time. The last poem in the cycle, 'Les Litanies de Satan' ('Litany to Satan'), is by virtue of its theological content, the miserere of an ophiolatrous liturgy. Satan appears with his Luciferian halo, as the keeper of profound knowledge, as an instructor in Promethean skills, as the patron saint of the stubborn and unyielding. From between the lines flashes the dark head of Blanqui.

> Toi qui fais au proscrit ce regard calme et haut
> Qui damne tout un peuple autour d'un échafaud.[31]

> (Thou givest to the Guilty their calm mien
> Which damns the crowd around the guillotine.)

translated by James Elroy Flecker

This Satan, whom the chain of invocations also knows as the 'father confessor . . . of the conspirators', is different from the infernal

---

reproduction at all. The public prosecutors of the Second Empire understood this, and so do their successors. Baron Seillière indicates this with a great deal of nonchalance in his interpretation of the first poem in the series *Révolte*. It is entitled 'Le Reniement de Saint Pierre' ('The Denial of Saint Peter') and includes the following verses:

> Rêvais-tu de ces jours . . .

> Où, le coeur tout gonflé d'espoir et de vaillance,
> Tu fouettais tous ces vils marchands à tour de bras,
> Où tu fus maître enfin? Le remords n'a-t-il pas
> Pénétré dans ton flanc plus avant que la lance?   (I, 136.)

> (Did you dream of those days . . .

> When whirling your whips, and full of valiant force,
> The moneylenders quailed at your advance:
> When you, in short, were master? Did remorse
> Not pierce your body further than the lance?)

translated by Roy Campbell

In this remorse the ironic interpreter sees self-reproaches for 'having missed such a good opportunity to establish the dictatorship of the proletariat' (Ernest Seillière, *Baudelaire*, Paris, 1931, p. 193).

31. I, 138.

intriguer who is called *Satan trismegistos*, the demon, in the poems, and appears in the prose pieces as His Highness who has his subterranean dwelling in the vicinity of the boulevard. Lemaître has pointed out the dichotomy which makes of the devil 'in one place the author of all evil and then again the great vanquished, the great victim'.[32] It is merely a different view of the problem if one asks what impelled Baudelaire to give a radical-theological form to his radical rejection of those in power.

After the defeat of the proletariat in the June fights, the protest against the bourgeois ideas of order and respectability was better preserved by the ruling classes than by the oppressed. Those who espoused freedom and justice saw in Napoleon III not the soldier king that he wanted to be in succession to his uncle, but a confidence man favoured by fortune. This is how his figure is preserved in the *Châtiments*. The *bohème dorée*, for its part, saw in his sumptuous feasts and the splendour with which he surrounded himself a realization of their dreams of a 'free' life. The memoirs of Count Viel-Castel in which he described the Emperor's surroundings make a Mimi and a Schaunard appear quite respectable and philistine by comparison. Among the upper classes, cynicism was part of the accepted style; in the lower classes, a rebellious argumentativeness was the norm. In his *Eloa* Vigny had, in the tradition of Byron, paid homage to Lucifer, the fallen angel, in the gnostic sense. Barthélémy, on the other hand, in his *Némésis* had associated Satanism with the ruling classes; he had a mass *des agios* celebrated and a psalm about annuities sung.[33] Baudelaire was thoroughly familiar with this dual aspect of Satan. To him, Satan spoke not only for the upper crust but for the lower classes as well. Marx could hardly have wished for a better reader of the following lines from the *Eighteenth Brumaire*: 'When the Puritans complained at the Council of Constance about the wicked lives of the popes . . . Cardinal Pierre d'Ailly thundered at them: "Only the devil incarnate can save the Catholic church, and you demand angels." Thus the French bourgeoisie cried after the *coup d'état*: "Only the head of the

32. Jules Lemaître, *Les contemporains, IVe série*, Paris, 1895, p. 30.
33. Cf. Auguste-Marseille Barthélémy, *Némésis, Satire hebdomadaire*, Paris, 1834, vol. 1, p. 225 ('L'archevêché et la bourse').

Society of the Tenth of December can save bourgeois society! Only theft can save property, perjury can save religion, bastardy the family, and disorder order." '[34] Even in his rebellious hours Baudelaire, the admirer of the Jesuits, did not wish to renounce this saviour completely and forever. His verses hold in reserve what his prose had not denied itself; that is why Satan appears in them. To him they owe their subtle power not to deny loyalty entirely, even in desperate outcries, to that which understanding and humaneness rebelled against. Almost always the confession of piousness comes from Baudelaire like a battle cry. He will not give up his Satan. He is the real stake in the struggle which Baudelaire had to carry on with his unbelief. It is not a matter of sacraments and prayers, but of the Luciferian privilege of blaspheming the Satan to whom one is addicted.

Baudelaire intended his friendship with Pierre Dupont to indicate that he was a social poet. The critical writings of d'Aurevilly contain a sketch of that author: 'In this talent and this mind, Cain has the upper hand over the gentle Abel – the brutal, starved, envious, wild Cain who has gone to the cities to consume the sediment of rancour which has accumulated in them and participate in the false ideas which experience their triumph there.'[35] This characterization expresses exactly what gave Baudelaire solidarity with Dupont. Like Cain, Dupont had 'gone to the cities' and turned away from the idyllic. 'He has absolutely no connection with poems as our fathers conceived of them . . . even with simple romances.'[36] Dupont sensed the approaching crisis of lyric poetry with the increasing rift between the city and the country. One of his verses contains an awkward admission of this; Dupont says that the poet 'alternately lends his ear to the forests and to the masses'. The masses rewarded him for his attention; around 1848 Dupont was the talk of the town. When the achievements of the Revolution were lost, one after another, Dupont wrote his *Chant du vote*. There are few things in the political literature of the time that are a match

34. Marx, *Der achtzehnte Brumaire des Louis Bonaparte*, op. cit., p. 124.

35. Jules-Amédée Barbey d'Aurevilly, *Le XIXe siècle. Les oeuvres et les hommes. 1re sèrie, 3e partie: Les poètes*, Paris, 1862, p. 242.

36. Pierre Larousse, *Dictionnaire universel du XIXe siècle*, vol. 6, Paris, 1870, p. 1413 (Article on Dupont).

to its refrain. It is a leaf of that laurel which Karl Marx claimed for the 'threateningly dark brows'[37] of the June fighters.

> Fais voir, en déjouant la ruse
> O Républicain à ces pervers
> Ta grande face de Méduse
> Au milieu de rouges éclairs.[38]

> (In foiling their tricks, show these evil-doers, O Republican, your great Medusa face surrounded by flashes of red lightning.)

The introduction which Baudelaire contributed to a collection of Dupont's poetry in 1851 was an act of literary strategy. In it may be found the following remarkable statement: 'The puerile utopia of the school of *l'art pour l'art* excluded morality and often even passion, and this necessarily made it sterile.' And with an obvious reference to Auguste Barbier he goes on to say: 'When a poet appeared who, despite occasional ineptitude, almost always proved to be great, and who in flaming language proclaimed the sacredness of the 1830 insurrection and sung the misery of England and Ireland . . . the question was settled once and for all and henceforth art was inseparable from both morality and utility.'[39] This has nothing of the profound duplicity which animates Baudelaire's own poetry. It supported the oppressed, though it espoused their illusions as well as their cause. It had an ear for the chants of the revolution and also for the 'higher voice' which spoke from the drumroll of the executions. When Bonaparte came to power through a *coup d'état*, Baudelaire was momentarily enraged. 'Then he looked at events from a "providential point of view" and subjected himself like a monk.'[40] 'Theocracy and communism'[41] were to him not convictions but insinuations which vied for his attention; the one was not as Seraphic and the other not as Luciferian as he probably thought. It did not take long for Baudelaire to abandon his revolutionary manifesto, and a number of years later he wrote:

37. Marx, *Dem Andenken der Junikämpfer*, cf. Riazanov, ed., *Karl Marx als Denker, Mensch und Revolutionär*, Vienna, 1928, p. 40.

38. Pierre Dupont, *Le chant du vote*, Paris, 1850.   39. II, 403ff.

40. Paul Desjardins, 'Charles Baudelaire', in *La revue bleue*, Paris, 1887, p. 19.   41. II, 659.

'Dupont owed his first poems to the grace and feminine delicacy of his nature. Fortunately the revolutionary activity which in those days carried almost everyone away did not entirely deflect him from his *natural* course.'[42] His abrupt break with *l'art pour l'art* was of value to Baudelaire only as an attitude. It permitted him to announce the latitude which was at his disposal as a man of letters. In this he was ahead of the writers of his time, including the greatest. This makes it evident in what respects he was above the literary activity surrounding him.

For a century and a half the literary life of the day had been centred around periodicals. Towards the end of the third decade of the century this began to change. The *feuilleton* provided a market for *belles-lettres* in the daily newspaper. The introduction of this cultural section summed up the changes which the July Revolution had brought to the press. In the restoration period single copies of newspapers could not be sold; people had to subscribe to a paper. Anyone who could not pay the high price of eighty francs for a year's subscription had to go to a café where often several people stood around reading one copy. In 1824 there were 47,000 subscribers to newspapers in Paris; in 1836 there were 70,000 and in 1846, 200,000. In this rise Girardin's paper *La Presse* had played a decisive part. It had brought about three important innovations: the decrease of the subscription to forty francs, advertisements, and the serial novel. At the same time, short, abrupt news items began to compete with detailed reports. These news items caught on because they could be employed commercially. The so-called '*réclame*' paved the way for them; this was an apparently independent notice which was actually paid for by a publisher and appeared in the editorial section of the newspaper, referring to a book for which an advertisement had appeared the day before or was printed in the same issue. As early as 1839 Sainte-Beuve complained about the demoralizing effect of the *réclame*: 'How could they damn a product [in a critique] about which it was said two inches below that it was a miracle of the epoch? The attraction of the ever-increasing type in which the advertisements were printed gained the upper hand; they constituted a magnetic mountain

42. II, 555.

which deflected the compass.'[43] The *réclame* was at the beginning of a development whose end were the stock-exchange notices that appeared in the journals and were paid for by interested persons. It is hardly possible to write a history of information separately from a history of the corruption of the press.

These informative items required little space. They and not the political editorials or the serialized novels enabled a newspaper to have a different look every day, an appearance that was cleverly varied when the pages were made up and constituted part of the paper's attractiveness. These items had to be constantly replenished. City gossip, theatrical intrigues, and 'things worth knowing' were their most popular sources. Their intrinsic cheap elegance, a quality that became so characteristic of the *feuilleton* section, was in evidence from the beginning. In her *Letters from Paris* Mme de Girardin welcomed photography as follows: 'At present much attention is being paid to Mr Daguerre's invention, and nothing is more comical than the serious elucidations which our salon scholars are giving of it. Mr Daguerre need not worry; no one is going to steal his secret from him. . . . Truly, his invention is wonderful; but people do not understand it, there have been too many explanations of it.'[44] The *feuilleton* style was not accepted immediately or everywhere. In 1860 and 1868 the two volumes of the *Revues parisiennes* by Baron Gaston de Flotte appeared in Marseille and Paris. They set themselves the task of combating the carelessness with which historical information was given, particularly in the *feuilleton* section of the Parisian press. The news fillers originated in cafés, over apéritifs. 'The custom of taking an apéritif . . . arose with the boulevard press. When there were only the large, serious papers . . . cocktail hours were unknown. The cocktail hour is the logical consequence of the "Paris timetable" and of city gossip.'[45] Coffee-house life habituated the editors to the rhythm of the news service even before its machinery had been developed. When the electrical telegraph came into use towards the end of the Second Empire, the

43. Sainte-Beuve, 'De la littérature industrielle', in *Revue des deux mondes*, 1839, pp. 682ff.

44. Mme Emile de Girardin (Delphine Gay), *Oeuvres complètes*, vol. 4: *Lettres parisiennes, 1836–1840*, Paris, 1860, pp. 289ff.

45. Gabriel Guillemot, *La bohème*, Paris, 1868, p. 72.

boulevards had lost their monopoly. News of accidents and crimes could now be obtained from all over the world.

The assimilation of a man of letters to the society in which he lived took place on the boulevard in the following fashion. On the boulevard he kept himself in readiness for the next incident, witticism, or rumour. There he unfolded the full fabric of his connections with colleagues and men-about-town, and he was as much dependent on their results as the cocottes were on their disguises.[46] On the boulevards he spent his hours of idleness which he displayed before people as part of his working hours. He behaved as if he had learned from Marx that the value of a commodity is determined by the working time socially necessary to produce it. In view of the protracted periods of idleness which in the eyes of the public were necessary for the realization of his own labour-power, its value became almost fantastic. This high valuation was not limited to the public. The high payments for *feuilletons* at that time indicate that they were founded in social conditions. There was in fact a connection between the decrease in the cost of newspaper subscriptions, the increase in advertising, and the growing importance of the *feuilleton* section.

'In the light of the new arrangements [the lowering of subscription rates] newspapers had to live on advertising revenues. . . . In order to obtain many advertisements, the quarter page which had become a poster had to be seen by as large a number of subscribers as possible. It was necessary to have a lure which was directed at all regardless of their private opinion and which served to replace politics with curiosity. . . . Once the point of departure, the subscription rate of 40 francs, existed, the progression was almost of necessity from advertisements to serialized novels.'[47] This very fact explains the high honorariums paid for such contributions. In 1845 Dumas signed a contract with the *Constitutionnel* and the *Presse* according to which he was given a minimum annual payment of

46. 'It does not take much acuteness to recognize that a girl who at eight o'clock may be seen sumptuously dressed in an elegant costume is the same who appears as a shop girl at nine o'clock and as a peasant girl at ten' (F.-F.-A. Béraud, *Les filles publiques de Paris et la police qui les régit*, Paris–Leipzig, 1839, vol. 1, pp. 51ff.).

47. Alfred Nettement, *Histoire de la littérature française sous le Gouvernement de Juillet*, Paris, 1859, vol. 1, pp. 301ff.

63,000 francs for supplying at least eighteen volumes a year.[48] For his *Mystères de Paris* Eugène Sue received an advance of 100,000 francs. Lamartine's fees have been estimated at 5 million francs for the period from 1838 to 1851. He received 600,000 francs for his *Histoire des Girondins* which first appeared in the *feuilleton* section. The generous fees paid for everyday literary merchandise necessarily led to abuses. When publishers acquired manuscripts, they occasionally reserved the right to print them under the name of a writer of their choice. This was predicated on the fact that some successful novelists were not fussy about the use of their names. Some details about this may be found in a lampoon entitled *Fabrique de romans, Maison Alexandre Dumas et Cie.*[49] The *Revue des deux mondes* commented at that time: 'Who knows the titles of all the books written by Mr Dumas? Does he know them himself? Unless he keeps a ledger with a "Debit" and a "Credit" side, he surely has forgotten more than one of his legitimate, illegitimate, or adopted children.'[50] It was said that Dumas employed in his basements a whole army of poor writers. As late as 1855, ten years after this commentary by the great review, a small organ of the *bohème* printed the following picturesque scene from the life of a successful novelist whom the author calls de Sanctis: 'When he arrived home, Mr de Sanctis carefully locked the door . . . and opened a small door hidden behind his books. He found himself in a rather dirty, poorly lit little room in which sat a man with dishevelled hair who looked sullen but obsequious and had a long goose-quill in his hand. Even from a distance one could recognize him as a born novelist, though he is only a former employee of a ministry who has learned the art of Balzac from reading the *Constitutionnel*. He is the real author of *The Chamber of Skulls*; he is the novelist.'[51] During the Second

48. Cf. S. Charléty, 'La monarchie de Juillet', in Ernest Lavisse, *Histoire de France contemporaine depuis la Révolution jusqu'à la paix de 1919*, Paris, 1921–2, vol. 4, p. 352.

49. cf. Eugène de (Jacquot) Mirecourt, *Fabrique de romans. Maison Alexandre Dumas et Cie*, Paris, 1845.

50. Paulin Limayrac, 'Du roman actuel et de nos romanciers', in *Revue des deux mondes*, 1845, pp. 953ff.

51. Paul Saulnier, 'Du roman en général et du romancier moderne en particulier', in *La bohème*, 1855, I, p. 3. The use of 'ghosts' was not confined

Republic, parliament tried to combat the proliferation of the *feuilleton*; each instalment of a serialized novel was taxed one centime. After a short time this regulation was rescinded by the reactionary press laws which curtailed freedom of opinion and thus enhanced the value of the *feuilleton*.

The high fees paid for *feuilletons* coupled with their large market helped the writers who supplied them to achieve a great reputation. It was natural for an individual to exploit his reputation together with his financial resources; a political career opened up for him almost automatically. This led to new forms of corruption, and they were more consequential than the misuse of well-known writers' names. Once the political ambition of a writer had been aroused, it was natural for the regime to show him the right road. In 1846 Salvandy, the Minister of Colonies, invited Alexandre Dumas to take a trip to Tunis at government expense – estimated at 10,000 francs – to publicize the colonies. The expedition was unsuccessful, cost a lot of money, and ended with a small inquiry in the Chamber of Deputies. Sue had more luck; on the strength of the success of his *Mystères de Paris* he not only increased the number of subscribers to the *Constitutionnel* from 3,600 to 20,000, but was elected a deputy in 1850 with the votes of 130,000 Parisian workingmen. It was not much of a gain for the proletarian voters; Marx called his election 'a sentimental commentary'[52] on the seats previously won. If literature was able to open a political career to favoured writers, this career in turn may be used for a critical evaluation of their writings. Lamartine constitutes a case in point.

Lamartine's decisive successes, the *Méditations* and the *Harmonies*, go back to a time when the French peasants were still able to enjoy the fruits of their labours on the land. In a naive poem addressed to Alphonse Karr, the poet equated his creativity with that of a wine-grower:

> Tout homme avec fierté peut vendre sa sueur!
> Je vends ma grappe en fruit comme tu vends ta fleur,
> Heureux quand son nectar, sous mon pied qui la foule,
> Dans mes tonneaux nombreux en ruisseaux d'ambre coule,

to serialized novels. Scribe employed a number of anonymous collaborators for the dialogue of his plays.

52. Marx, *Der achtzehnte Brumaire des Louis Bonaparte*, op. cit., p. 68.

> Produisant à son maître ivre de sa cherté,
> Beaucoup d'or pour payer beaucoup de liberté![53]

> (Every man with pride can sell his sweat! I sell my bunch of grapes as you your flowers, happy when its nectar, under my foot which tramples it, flows in many casks with streams of amber, producing for its master, drunk with his quality, a lot of gold to pay for a lot of freedom!)

These lines, in which Lamartine praises his prosperity as rustic, and boasts of the fees which his product gets him on the market, are revealing if one reads them less from the viewpoint of morality[54] than as an expression of Lamartine's class feeling – that of a peasant with a plot of land. This is part of the history of Lamartine's poetry. In the 1840s the situation of the peasant with a plot of land had become critical. He was in debt; his plot 'no longer lay in the so-called fatherland, but in the register of mortgages'.[55] This meant the decline of rustic optimism, the basis of the transfiguring view of nature which is characteristic of Lamartine's poetry. 'But while the newly-created small holding, in its harmony with society, its dependence on the forces of nature and its subjection to the authority which protected it from above was naturally religious, the small holding ruined by debts, at odds with society and authority and driven beyond its own limits, naturally becomes irreligious. Heaven was quite a nice supplement to the newly-gained narrow strip of land, especially because it makes the weather; it becomes an insult when it is forced on people as a substitute for the plot of land.'[56] Lamartine's poems had been cloud formations on that very heaven. As Sainte-Beuve wrote in 1830, 'The poetry of André Chénier . . . is, so to speak, the landscape over which Lamartine

53. Alphonse de Lamartine, 'Lettre à Alphonse Karr', in *Oeuvres poétiques complètes*, edited by Guyard, Paris, 1963, p. 1506.

54. In an open letter to Lamartine the ultramontanist Louis Veuillot wrote: 'Could it be that you really don't know that "to be free" really means to despise gold? And in order to obtain the kind of freedom that is bought with gold you produce your books in the same commercial fashion as you produce your vegetables or your wine!' (Louis Veuillot, *Pages choisies*, edited by Albalat, Lyons, 1906, p. 31.)

55. Marx, op. cit., p. 123.

56. ibid., p. 122.

has spread the heavens.'[57] This heaven collapsed forever when in 1848 the French peasants voted for Bonaparte as president. Lamartine had helped prepare that vote.[58] Sainte-Beuve wrote about Lamartine's role in the revolution: 'He probably never thought that he was destined to become the Orpheus who was to guide and moderate that incursion of the barbarians with his golden bow.'[59] Baudelaire dryly calls him 'a bit whorish, a bit prostituted'.[60]

Hardly anyone had a keener eye for the problematical sides of this splendid figure than Baudelaire. This may be due to the fact that he himself had always felt little splendour attaching to his own person. Porché believes it looks as though Baudelaire had no choice about where he could place his manuscripts.[61] Ernest Raynaud writes: 'Baudelaire had to be prepared for unethical practices. He was dealing with publishers who counted on the vanity of sophisticated people, amateurs, and beginners, and who accepted manuscripts only if a subscription was entered.'[62] Baudelaire's own conduct is in keeping with this state of affairs. He offered the same manuscript to several papers at the same time and authorized reprints without indicating them as such. From his early period on he viewed the literary market without any illusions. In 1846 he wrote: 'No matter how beautiful a house may be, it is, primarily and before one dwells on its beauty, so and so many metres high and so and so many metres long. In the same way, literature, which

57. Sainte-Beuve, *Vie, poésies et pensées de Joseph Delorme*, Paris, 1863, p. 170.

58. On the basis of reports from Kisselyev, the then Russian ambassador in Paris, Pokrewski has demonstrated that things happened as Marx had outlined them in his *Class Struggles in France*. On 6 April 1849 Lamartine had assured the ambassador that he would concentrate troops in the capital – a measure which the bourgeoisie later attempted to justify with the workers' demonstrations of 16 April. Lamartine's remark that it would take him about ten days to concentrate the troops indeed puts those demonstrations in an ambiguous light (cf. Michail N. Pokrewski, *Historische Aufsätze*, Vienna, 1928, pp. 108ff.).

59. Sainte-Beuve, *Les consolations*, p. 118.

60. Quoted in Françoise Porché, *La vie douloureuse de Charles Baudelaire*, Paris, 1926, p. 248.

61. ibid., p. 156.

62. Ernest Raynaud, *Charles Baudelaire*, Paris, 1922, p. 319.

constitutes the most inestimable substance, is primarily a matter of filling up lines; and a literary architect whose mere name does not promise a profit must sell at any price.'[63] To his end Baudelaire remained in a bad position on the literary market. It has been calculated that he earned no more than 15,000 francs from his entire work.

'Balzac is ruining himself with coffee, Musset is dulling himself by drinking absinthe. . . . Murger is dying in a sanatorium, as is now Baudelaire. And not one of these writers has been a Socialist!'[64] Thus wrote Sainte-Beuve's private secretary, Jules Troubat. Baudelaire surely deserved the recognition intended by the last sentence. But this does not mean that he lacked insight into the true situation of a man of letters. He frequently compared such a man, and first of all himself, with a whore. His sonnet to the venal muse – 'La Muse vénale' – speaks of this. The great introductory poem, 'Au Lecteur', presents the poet in the unflattering position of someone who takes cold cash for his confession. One of his earliest poems, among those which were not included in the *Fleurs du mal*, is addressed to a streetwalker. This is its second stanza:

> Pour avoir des souliers, elle a vendu son âme;
> Mais le bon Dieu rirait si, près de cette infâme,
> Je trenchais du tartufe et singeais la hauteur,
> Moi qui vends ma pensée et qui veux être auteur.[65]

> (In order to have shoes she has sold her soul; but the Good Lord would laugh if, close to that vile person, I played the hypocrite and mimicked loftiness, I who sell my thought and want to be an author.)

The second stanza, 'Cette bohème-là, c'est mon tout', nonchalantly includes this creature in the brotherhood of the *bohème*. Baudelaire knew what the true situation of the man of letters was: he goes to the marketplace as a *flâneur*, supposedly to take a look at it, but in reality to find a buyer.

63. II, 385.
64. Quoted in Eugène Crépet, *Charles Baudelaire*, Paris, 1906, pp. 196ff.
65. I, 209.

II. The *Flâneur*

Once a writer had entered the marketplace, he looked around as in a diorama. A special literary genre has preserved his first attempts at orienting himself. It is a panorama literature. It was not by chance that *Le Livre des cent-et-un*, *Les Français peints par eux-mêmes*, *Le Diable à Paris*, *La Grande Ville* enjoyed the favour of the capital city at the same time as the dioramas. These books consist of individual sketches which, as it were, reproduce the plastic foreground of those panoramas with their anecdotal form and the extensive background of the panoramas with their store of information. Numerous authors contributed to these volumes. Thus these anthologies are products of the same belletristic collective work for which Girardin had procured an outlet in the *feuilleton*. They were the salon attire of a literature which fundamentally was designed to be sold in the streets. In this literature, the modest-looking, paperbound, pocket-size volumes called 'physiologies' had pride of place. They investigated types that might be encountered by a person taking a look at the marketplace. From the itinerant street vendor of the boulevards to the dandy in the foyer of the opera-house, there was not a figure of Paris life that was not sketched by a *physiologue*. The great period of the genre came in the early forties. It was the *haute école* of the *feuilleton*; Baudelaire's generation went through it. The fact that it meant little to Baudelaire himself indicates the early age at which he went his own way.

In 1841 there were seventy-six new physiologies.[1] After that year the genre declined, and it disappeared together with the reign

1. cf. Charles Louandre, 'Statistique littéraire de la production intellectuelle

of the citizen-king Louis-Philippe. It was a basically petty-bourgeois genre. Monnier, its master, was a philistine endowed with an uncommon capacity for self-observation. Nowhere did these physiologies break through the most limited horizon. After the types had been covered, the physiology of the city had its turn. There appeared *Paris la nuit, Paris à table, Paris dans l'eau, Paris à cheval, Paris pittoresque, Paris marié*. When this vein, too, was exhausted, a 'physiology' of the nations was attempted. Nor was the 'physiology' of the animals neglected, for animals have always been an innocuous subject. Innocuousness was of the essence. In his studies on the history of caricature, Eduard Fuchs points out that the beginning of the physiologies coincided with the so-called September Laws, the tightened censorship of 1836. These laws summarily forced a team of able artists with a background in satire out of politics. If that could be done in the graphic arts, the government's manoeuvre was bound to be all the more successful in literature, for there was no political energy there that could compare with that of a Daumier. Reaction, then, was the principle 'which explains the colossal parade of bourgeois life which . . . began in France. . . . Everything passed in review. . . . Days of celebration and days of mourning, work and play, conjugal customs and bachelors' practices, the family, the home, children, school, society, the theatre, types, professions.'[2]

The leisurely quality of these descriptions fits the style of the *flâneur* who goes botanizing on the asphalt. But even in those days it was not possible to stroll about everywhere in the city. Before Haussmann wide pavements were rare, and the narrow ones afforded little protection from vehicles. Strolling could hardly have assumed the importance it did without the arcades. 'The arcades, a rather recent invention of industrial luxury,' so says an illustrated guide to Paris of 1852, 'are glass-covered, marble-panelled passageways through entire complexes of houses whose proprietors have combined for such speculations. Both sides of these passageways, which

en France depuis quinze ans', in *Revue des deux mondes*, 15 November 1847, pp. 686ff.

2. Eduard Fuchs, *Die Karikatur der europäischen Völker*, Munich, 1921, vol. 1, p. 362.

are lighted from above, are lined with the most elegant shops, so that such an arcade is a city, even a world, in miniature.' It is in this world that the *flâneur* is at home; he provides 'the favourite sojourn of the strollers and the smokers, the stamping ground of all sorts of little *métiers*',[3] with its chronicler and its philosopher. As for himself, he obtains there the unfailing remedy for the kind of boredom that easily arises under the baleful eyes of a satiated reactionary regime. In the words of Guys as quoted by Baudelaire, 'Anyone who is capable of being bored in a crowd is a blockhead. I repeat: a blockhead, and a contemptible one.'[4] The arcades were a cross between a street and an *intérieur*. If one can speak of an artistic device of the physiologies, it is the proven device of the *feuilleton*, namely, to turn a boulevard into an *intérieur*. The street [4a] becomes a dwelling for the *flâneur*; he is as much at home among the façades of houses as a citizen is in his four walls. To him the shiny, enamelled signs of businesses are at least as good a wall ornament as an oil painting is to a bourgeois in his salon. The walls are the desk against which he presses his notebooks; news-stands are his libraries and the terraces of cafés are the balconies from which he looks down on his household after his work is done. That life in all its variety and inexhaustible wealth of variations can thrive only among the grey cobblestones and against the grey background of despotism was the political secret on which the physiologies were based.

These writings were socially dubious, too. The long series of eccentric or simple, attractive or severe figures which the physiologies presented to the public in character sketches had one thing in common: they were harmless and of perfect bonhomie. Such a view of one's fellow man was so remote from experience that there were bound to be uncommonly weighty motives for it. The reason was an uneasiness of a special sort. People had to adapt themselves to a new and rather strange situation, one that is peculiar to big cities. Simmel has felicitously formulated what was involved here. 'Someone who sees without hearing is much more uneasy than someone

3. Ferdinand von Gall, *Paris und seine Salons*, Oldenburg, 1845, vol. 2, pp. 22ff.

4. II, 333.

[4a. In the preceding sentence, the original word 'street' was later replaced by 'boulevard'. *Editorial note in the German edition.*]

who hears without seeing. In this there is something characteristic of the sociology of the big city. Interpersonal relationships in big cities are distinguished by a marked preponderance of the activity of the eye over the activity of the ear. The main reason for this is the public means of transportation. Before the development of buses, railroads, and trams in the nineteenth century, people had never been in a position of having to look at one another for long minutes or even hours without speaking to one another.'[5] This new situation was, as Simmel recognized, not a pleasant one. In his *Eugene Aram*, Bulwer-Lytton orchestrated his description of big-city dwellers with a reference to Goethe's remark that every person, the best as well as the most wretched, carries around a secret which would make him hateful to all others if it became known.[6] The physiologies were designed to brush such disquieting notions aside as insignificant. They constituted, so to speak, the blinkers of the 'narrow-minded city animal' which Marx wrote about.[7] A description of the proletarian in Foucaud's *Physiologie de l'industrie fran- çaise* shows what a thoroughly limited vision these physiologies offered when the need arose: 'Quiet enjoyment is almost ex- hausting for a workingman. The house in which he lives may be surrounded by greenery under a cloudless sky, it may be fragrant with flowers and enlivened by the chirping of birds; but if a worker is idle, he will remain inaccessible to the charms of solitude. How- ever, if a loud noise or a whistle from a distant factory happens to hit his ear, if he so much as hears the monotonous clattering of the machines in a factory, his face immediately brightens. He no longer feels the choice fragrance of flowers. The smoke from the tall fac- tory chimney, the booming blows on the anvil, make him tremble with joy. He remembers the happy days of his work that was guided by the spirit of the inventor.'[8] An entrepreneur who read this description may have gone to bed more relaxed than was his wont.

It was indeed the most obvious thing to give people a friendly

5. Georg Simmel, *Soziologie*, 4th edn, Berlin, 1958, p. 486.

6. cf. Bulwer-Lytton, *Eugene Aram. A Tale*, Paris, 1832, p. 314.

7. Marx and Engels on Feuerbach, in *Marx-Engels-Archiv, Zeitschrift des Marx-Engels-Instituts*, edited by David Riazanov, Frankfurt, 1926, vol. 1, pp. 271ff.

8. Edouard Foucaud, *Paris inventeur. Physiologie de l'industrie française*, Paris, 1844, pp. 222ff.

picture of one another. Thus the physiologies helped fashion the
phantasmagoria of Parisian life in their own way. But their method
could not get them very far. People knew one another as debtors
and creditors, salesmen and customers, employers and employees,
and above all as competitors. In the long run it did not seem very
likely that they could be made to believe their associates were
harmless oddballs. Therefore these writings soon developed another
view of the matter which rang true to a far greater extent. They
went back to the physiognomists of the eighteenth century, although they had little to do with the more solid endeavours of the
latter. In Lavater or in Gall there was, next to the speculative and
the visionary, genuine empiricism. The physiologies lived on the
credit of this empiricism without adding anything of their own.
They assured people that everyone was, unencumbered by any
factual knowledge, able to make out the profession, the character,
the background, and the life-style of passers-by. In these writings
this ability appears as a gift which a good fairy bestows upon an
inhabitant of a big city at birth. With such certainties Balzac, more
than anyone else, was in his element. His predilection for unquali-
fied statements was served well by them. 'Genius,' he wrote, 'is so
visible in a person that even the least educated man walking around
in Paris will, when he comes across a great artist, know immediately
what he has found.'[9] Delvau, Baudelaire's friend and the most
interesting among the minor masters of the *feuilleton*, claimed that
he could divide the Parisian public according to its various strata
as easily as a geologist distinguishes the layers in rocks. If that sort
of thing could be done, then, to be sure, life in the big city was not
nearly so disquieting as it probably seemed to people. Then these
questions by Baudelaire were just empty phrases: 'What are the
dangers of the forest and the prairie compared with the daily shocks
and conflicts of civilization? Whether a man grabs his victim on
a boulevard or stabs his quarry in unknown woods – does he
not remain both here and there the most perfect of all beasts of
prey?'[10]

For this victim Baudelaire uses the expression '*dupe*'; the word
refers to someone who is cheated or fooled, and such a person is the

9. Honoré de Balzac, *Le cousin Pons*, Paris, 1914, p. 130.
10. II, 637.

antithesis of a connoisseur of human nature. The more uncanny a big city becomes, the more knowledge of human nature – so it was thought – it takes to operate in it. In actuality, the intensified struggle for survival led an individual to make an imperious proclamation of his interests. When it is a matter of evaluating a person's behaviour, an intimate acquaintance with these interests will often be much more useful than an acquaintance with his personality. The ability of which the *flâneur* likes to boast is, therefore, more likely to be one of the idols Bacon already located in the marketplace. Baudelaire hardly paid homage to this idol. His belief in original sin made him immune to a belief in a knowledge of human nature. He sided with de Maistre who, for his part, had combined a study of dogma with a study of Bacon.

The soothing little remedies which the physiologists offered for sale were soon passé. On the other hand, the literature which concerned itself with the disquieting and threatening aspects of urban life was to have a great future. This literature, too, dealt with the masses, but its method was different from that of the physiologies. It cared little about the definition of types; rather, it investigated the functions which are peculiar to the masses in a big city. One of these claimed particular attention; it had been emphasized by a police report as early as the turn of the nineteenth century. 'It is almost impossible,' wrote a Parisian secret agent in 1798, 'to maintain good behaviour in a thickly populated area where an individual is, so to speak, unknown to all others and thus does not have to blush in front of anyone.'[11] Here the masses appear as the asylum that shields an asocial person from his persecutors. Of all the menacing aspects of the masses, this one became apparent first. It is at the origin of the detective story.

In times of terror, when everyone is something of a conspirator, everybody will be in a situation where he has to play detective. Strolling gives him the best prospects of doing so. Baudelaire wrote: 'An observer is a *prince* who is everywhere in possession of his incognito.'[12] If the *flâneur* is thus turned into an unwilling detective,

11. Quoted in Adolphe Schmidt, *Tableaux de la revolution française, publiées sur les papiers inédits du département et de la police secrète de Paris,* vol. 3, Leipzig, 1870, p. 337.

12. II, 333.

it does him a lot of good socially, for it accredits his idleness. He only seems to be indolent, for behind this indolence there is the watchfulness of an observer who does not take his eyes off a miscreant. Thus the detective sees rather wide areas opening up to his self-esteem. He develops forms of reaction that are in keeping with the pace of a big city. He catches things in flight; this enables him to dream that he is like an artist. Everyone praises the swift crayon of the graphic artist. Balzac claims that artistry as such is tied to a quick grasp.[13]

Criminological sagacity coupled with the pleasant nonchalance of the *flâneur* – that is the outline of Dumas' *Mohicans de Paris*. The hero of this book decides to go forth in search of adventure by following a scrap of paper which he has given to the wind to play with. No matter what trail the *flâneur* may follow, every one of them will lead him to a crime. This is an indication of how the detective story, regardless of its sober calculations, also participates in fashioning the phantasmagoria of Parisian life. As yet it does not glorify the criminal, though it does glorify his adversaries and, above all, the hunting-grounds where they pursue him. Messac has shown how an attempt has been made to bring in reminiscences of Cooper.[14] The most interesting thing about Cooper's influence is that it is not concealed but displayed. In the above-mentioned *Mohicans de Paris* this display is in the very title; the author promises the reader that he will open a tropical forest and a prairie for him in Paris. The woodcut used as a frontispiece in the third volume shows a bushy street which was little frequented at that time; the caption under this picture reads: 'The tropical forest in the Rue d'Enfer.' The publisher's leaflet for this volume outlines the connection in a magnificent phrase in which one may see an expression of the author's enthusiasm for himself: 'Paris – the Mohicans . . . these two names clash like the *qui vive* of two gigantic unknowns. An abyss separates the two; through it flashes a spark of that electric light which has its source in Alexandre Dumas.' Even

13. In his *Séraphita* Balzac speaks of 'a quick look whose perceptions in rapid succession placed the most antithetical landscapes of the earth at the disposal of the imagination'.

14. cf. Roger Messac, *Le 'Detectif novel' et l'influence de la pensée scientifique*, Paris, 1929.

earlier, Féval had involved a redskin in the adventures of a metropolis. This man is named Tovah, and on a ride in a fiacre he manages to scalp his four white companions in such a way that the coachman does not notice anything. At the very beginning, the *Mystères de Paris* refers to Cooper in promising that the book's heroes from the Parisian underworld 'are no less removed from civilization than the savages who are so splendidly depicted by Cooper'. But Balzac in particular never tired of referring to Cooper as his model. 'The poetry of terror of which the American woods with their hostile tribes on the warpath encountering each other are so full – this poetry which stood Cooper in such good stead attaches in the same way to the smallest details of Parisian life. The pedestrians, the shops, the hired coaches, or a man leaning against a window – all this was of the same burning interest to the members of Peyrade's bodyguard as a tree stump, a beaver's den, a rock, a buffalo skin, an immobile canoe, or a floating leaf was to the reader of a novel by Cooper.' Balzac's intrigue is rich in forms ranging from stories about Indians to detective stories. At an early date there were objections to his 'Mohicans in spencer jackets' and 'Hurons in frock coats'.[15] On the other hand, Hippolyte Babou, who was close to Baudelaire, wrote retrospectively in 1857: 'When Balzac breaks through walls to give free rein to observation, people listen at the doors. . . . In short, they behave, as our English neighbours in their prudery put it, like *police detectives*.'[16]

The detective story, whose interest lies in a logical construction that the crime story as such need not have, appeared in France for the first time in the form of translations of Poe's stories 'The Mystery of Marie Roget', 'The Murders in the Rue Morgue', and 'The Purloined Letter'. With his translations of these models, Baudelaire adopted the genre. Poe's work was definitely absorbed in his own, and Baudelaire emphasizes this fact by stating his solidarity with the method in which the individual genres that Poe embraced harmonize. Poe was one of the greatest technicians of modern literature. As Valéry pointed out,[17] he was the first to attempt the

15. cf. André Le Breton, *Balzac*, Paris, 1905, p. 83.
16. Hippolyte Babou, *La vérité sur le cas de M. Champfleury*, Paris, 1857, p. 30.
17. cf. Baudelaire, *Les Fleurs du mal*, Paris, 1928; introduction by Paul Valéry.

scientific story, a modern cosmogony, the description of patho-
logical phenomena. These genres he regarded as exact products of
a method for which he claimed universal validity. In this very point
Baudelaire sided with him, and in Poe's spirit he wrote: 'The time
is not distant when it will be understood that a literature which
refuses to make its way in brotherly concord with science and
philosophy is a murderous and suicidal literature.'[18] The detective
story, the most momentous among Poe's technical achievements,
was part of a literature that satisfied Baudelaire's postulate. Its
analysis constitutes part of the analysis of Baudelaire's own work,
despite the fact that Baudelaire wrote no stories of this type. The
Fleurs du mal have three of its decisive elements as *disjecta membra*:
the victim and the scene of the crime ('Une Martyre'), the murderer
('Le Vin de l'assassin'), the masses ('Le Crépuscule du soir'). The
fourth element is lacking – the one that permits the intellect to
break through this emotion-laden atmosphere. Baudelaire wrote no
detective story because, given the structure of his instincts, it was
impossible for him to identify with the detective. In him, the cal-
culating, constructive element was on the side of the asocial
and had become an integral part of cruelty. Baudelaire was too
good a reader of the Marquis de Sade to be able to compete with
Poe.[19]

The original social content of the detective story was the oblitera-
tion of the individual's traces in the big-city crowd. Poe concerns
himself with this motif in detail in 'The Mystery of Marie Roget',
the most voluminous of his detective stories. At the same time this
story is the prototype of the utilization of journalistic information
in the solution of crimes. Poe's detective, the Chevalier Dupin, here
works not with personal observation but with reports from the
daily press. The critical analysis of these reports constitutes the
rumour in the story. Among other things, the time of the crime has
to be established. One paper, *Le Commercial*, expresses the view
that Marie Roget, the murdered woman, has been done away with
immediately after she has left her mother's apartment. Poe writes:
' "It is impossible that a person so well known to thousands as this

18. II, 424.
19. 'One always has to go back to Sade . . . to explain evil' (II, 694).

young woman was, should have passed three blocks without some one having seen her." This is the idea of a man long resident in Paris – a public man – and one whose walks to and fro in the city have been mostly limited to the vicinity of the public offices. . . . He passes to and fro, at regular intervals, within a confined periphery, abounding in individuals who are led to observation of his person through interest in the kindred nature of his occupation with their own. But the walks of Marie may, in general, be supposed discursive. In this particular instance it will be understood as most probable that she proceeded upon a route of more than average diversity from her accustomed ones. The parallel which we imagine to have existed in the mind of *Le Commercial* would only be sustained in the event of the two individuals traversing the whole city. In this case, granting the personal acquaintances to be equal, the chances would be also equal that an equal number of personal *rencontres* would be made. For my own part, I should hold it not only as possible, but as far more than probable, that Marie might have proceeded, at any given period, by any one of the many routes between her own residence and that of her aunt, without meeting a single individual whom she knew, or by whom she was known. In viewing this question in its full and proper light, we must hold steadily in mind the great disproportion between the personal acquaintances of even the most noted individual in Paris, and the entire population of Paris itself.' If one disregards the context which gives rise to these reflections in Poe, the detective loses his competence, but the problem does not lose its validity. A variation of it forms the basis of one of the most famous poems in the *Fleurs du mal*, the sonnet entitled 'A une passante'.

> La rue assourdissante autour de moi hurlait.
> Longue, mince, en grand deuil, douleur majestueuse,
> Une femme passa, d'une main fastueuse
> Soulevant, balançant le feston et l'ourlet;
>
> Agile et noble, avec sa jambe de statue.
> Moi, je buvais, crispé comme un extravagant,
> Dans son oeil, ciel livide où germe l'ouragan,
> La douceur qui fascine et le plaisir qui tue.

Un éclair . . . puis la nuit! – Fugitive beauté
Dont le regard m'a fait soudainement renaître,
Ne te verrai-je plus que dans l'éternité?

Ailleurs, bien loin d'ici! trop tard! *jamais* peut-être!
Car j'ignore où tu fuis, tu ne sais où je vais,
O toi que j'eusse aimée, ô toi qui le savais![20]

To a Passer-by

Amid the deafening traffic of the town,
Tall, slender, in deep mourning, with majesty,
A woman passed, raising, with dignity
In her poised hand, the flounces of her gown;

Graceful, noble, with a statue's form.
And I drank, trembling as a madman thrills,
From her eyes, ashen sky· where brooded storm,
The softness that fascinates, the pleasure that kills.

A flash . . . then night! – O lovely fugitive,
I am suddenly reborn from your swift glance;
Shall I never see you till eternity?

Somewhere, far off! too late! *never*, perchance!
Neither knows where the other goes or lives;
We might have loved, and you knew this might be!

translated by C. F. MacIntyre

This sonnet presents the crowd not as the refuge of a criminal but as that of love which eludes the poet. One may say that it deals with the function of the crowd not in the life of the citizen but in the life of the erotic person. At first glance this function appears to be a negative one, but it is not. Far from eluding the erotic in the crowd, the apparition which fascinates him is brought to him by this very crowd. The delight of the city-dweller is not so much love at first sight as love at last sight. The *never* marks the high point of the encounter, when the poet's passion seems to be frustrated but in reality bursts out of him like a flame. He burns in this flame, but no Phoenix arises from it. The rebirth in the first tercet reveals a

20. I, 106.

view of the occurrence which in the light of the preceding stanza seems very problematical. What makes his body twitch spasmodically is not the excitement of a man in whom an image has taken possession of every fibre of his being; it partakes more of the shock with which an imperious desire suddenly overcomes a lonely man. The phrase *comme un extravagant* almost expresses this; the poet's emphasis on the fact that the female apparition is in mourning is not designed to conceal it. In reality there is a profound gulf between the quatrains which present the occurrence and the tercets which transfigure it. When Thibaudet says that these verses 'could only have been written in a big city',[21] he does not penetrate beneath their surface. The inner form of these verses is revealed in the fact that in them love itself is recognized as being stigmatized by the big city.[22]

Since the days of Louis-Philippe the bourgeoisie has endeavoured to compensate itself for the inconsequential nature of private life in the big city. It seeks such compensation within its four walls. Even if a bourgeois is unable to give his earthly being permanence, it seems to be a matter of honour with him to preserve the traces of his articles and requisites of daily use in perpetuity. The bourgeoisie cheerfully takes the impression of a host of objects. For slippers and pocket watches, thermometers and egg-cups, cutlery and umbrellas it tries to get covers and cases. It prefers velvet and plush covers which preserve the impression of every touch. For the Makart style, the style of the end of the Second Empire, a dwelling becomes a kind of casing. This style views it as a kind of case for a person and embeds him in it together with all his appurtenances, tending his traces as nature tends dead fauna embedded in granite. One should not fail to recognize that there are two sides to this process. The real or sentimental value of the objects thus preserved

21. Albert Thibaudet, *Intérieurs*, Paris, 1924, p. 22.

22. The motif of love for a woman passing by occurs in an early poem by Stefan George. The poet has missed the important thing: the stream in which the woman moves past, borne along by the crowd. The result is a self-conscious elegy. The poet's glances – so he must confess to his lady – have 'moved away, moist with longing/before they dared mingle with yours' (*'feucht vor sehnen fortgezogen/eh sie in deine sich zu tauchen trauten'*) (Stefan George, *Hymnen. Pilgerfahrten. Algabal*, seventh edn, Berlin, 1922, p. 23). Baudelaire leaves no doubt that *he* looked deep into the eyes of the passer-by.

is emphasized. They are removed from the profane eyes of non-owners, and in particular their outlines are blurred in a characteristic way. It is not strange that resistance to controls, something that becomes second nature to asocial persons, returns in the propertied bourgeoisie.

In such customs it is possible to see the dialectical illustration of a text which appeared in many instalments in the *Journal officiel*. As early as 1836 Balzac wrote in *Modeste Mignon*: 'Poor women of France! You would probably like to remain unknown in order to carry on your little romances. But how can you manage to do this in a civilization which registers the departure and the arrival of coaches in public places, counts letters and stamps them when they are posted and again when they are delivered, which provides houses with numbers and will soon have the whole country down to the smallest plot of land in its registers.'[23] Since the French Revolution an extensive network of controls had brought bourgeois life ever more tightly into its meshes. The numbering of houses in the big cities may be used to document the progressive standardization. Napoleon's administration had made it obligatory for Paris in 1805. In proletarian sections, to be sure, this simple police measure had encountered resistance. As late as 1864 it was reported about Saint-Antoine, the carpenters' section, that 'if one asks an inhabitant of this suburb what his address is, he will always give the name of his house and not its cold, official number'.[24] In the long run, of course, such resistance was of no avail against the endeavour to compensate by means of a multifarious web of registrations for the fact that the disappearance of people in the masses of the big cities leaves no traces. Baudelaire found this endeavour as much of an encroachment as did any criminal. On his flight from his creditors he went to cafés or reading circles. Sometimes he had two domiciles at the same time – but on days when the rent was due, he often spent the night at a third place with friends. So he roved about in the city which had long since ceased to be home for the *flâneur*. Every bed in which he lay down had become a *lit 'hasardeux'*[25] for

23. Balzac, *Modeste Mignon*, Editions du Siècle, Paris, 1850, p. 99.

24. Sigmund Engländer, *Geschichte der französischen Arbeiter-Associationen*, 4 parts, Hamburg, 1863–4, III, p. 126.

25. I, 115.

him. Crépet has counted fourteen Paris addresses for Baudelaire between 1842 and 1858.

Technical measures had to come to the aid of the administrative control process. In the early days of the process of identification, whose present standard derives from the Bertillon method, the identity of a person was established through his signature. The invention of photography was a turning point in the history of this process. It is no less significant for criminology than the invention of the printing press is for literature. Photography made it possible for the first time to preserve permanent and unmistakable traces of a human being. The detective story came into being when this most decisive of all conquests of a person's incognito had been accomplished. Since then the end of efforts to capture a man in his speech and actions has not been in sight.

Poe's famous tale 'The Man of the Crowd' is something like the X-ray picture of a detective story. In it, the drapery represented by crime has disappeared. The mere armature has remained: the pursuer, the crowd, and an unknown man who arranges his walk through London in such a way that he always remains in the middle of the crowd. This unknown man is the *flâneur*. That is how Baudelaire interpreted him when, in his essay on Guys, he called the *flâneur* 'l'homme des foules'. But Poe's description of this figure is devoid of the connivance which Baudelaire had for it. To Poe the *flâneur* was, above all, someone who does not feel comfortable in his own company. That is why he seeks out the crowd; the reason why he hides in it is probably close at hand. Poe purposely blurs the difference between the asocial person and the *flâneur*. The harder a man is to find, the more suspicious he becomes. Refraining from a prolonged pursuit, the narrator quietly sums up his insight as follows: 'This old man . . . is the type and the genius of deep crime. He refuses to be alone. *He is the man of the crowd.*'

The author does not demand the reader's interest in this man alone; his description of the crowd will claim at least as much interest, for documentary as well as artistic reasons. In both respects the crowd stands out. The first thing that strikes one is the rapt attention with which the narrator follows the spectacle of the crowd. This same spectacle is followed, in a well-known story by E. T. A. Hoffmann, by the 'Cousin at his corner window'. But this man, who is installed in his household, views the crowd with great constraint, whereas the man who stares through the window-panes of a coffeehouse has penetrating eyes. In the difference between the two observation posts lies the difference between Berlin and London. On the one hand there is the man of leisure. He sits in his alcove as in a box in the theatre; when he wants to take a closer look at the marketplace, he has opera glasses at hand. On the other hand there is the anonymous consumer who enters a café and will shortly leave it again, attracted by the magnet of the mass which constantly has him in its range. On the one side there is a multiplicity of little genre pictures which in their totality constitute an album of coloured engravings; on the other side there is a view which would be capable of inspiring a great etcher – an enormous crowd in which no one is either quite transparent or quite opaque to all others. A German petty bourgeois is subject to very narrow limits, and yet Hoffmann by nature belonged to the family of the Poes and the Baudelaires. In the biographical notes to the original edition of his last writings we read: 'Hoffmann was never especially fond of Nature. He valued people – communication with them, observations about them, merely seeing them – more than anything else. If he went for a walk in summer, something that he did every day toward evening in fine weather, there was hardly a wine tavern or a confectioner's shop where he did not stop in to see whether people were there and what people were there.'[26] At a later date, when Dickens went travelling, he repeatedly complained about the lack of street noises which were indispensable to him for his production. 'I cannot express how much I want these [the streets],' he wrote in 1846 from Lausanne while he was working on *Dombey and Son*. 'It seems as if they supplied something to my brain, which it cannot bear, when busy, to lose. For a week or a fortnight I can write prodigiously in a retired place . . . and a day in London sets me up again and starts me. But the toil and labour of writing, day after day, without that magic lantern, is *immense*. . . . *My* figures seem disposed to stagnate without crowds about them.'[27]

26. E. T. A. Hoffmann, *Ausgewählte Schriften*, vol. 15: *Leben und Nachlass* by Julius Eduard Hitzig, vol. 3, Stuttgart, 1839, pp. 32ff.

27. Franz Mehring, 'Charles Dickens', in *Die Neue Zeit*, 30 (1911–12),

Among the many things that Baudelaire found to criticize about hated Brussels, one thing filled him with particular rage: 'No shop-windows. Strolling, something that nations with imagination love, is not possible in Brussels. There is nothing to see, and the streets are unusable.'[28] Baudelaire loved solitude, but he wanted it in a crowd.

In the course of his story, Poe lets it grow dark. He lingers over the city by gaslight. The appearance of the street as an *intérieur* in which the phantasmagoria of the *flâneur* is concentrated is hard to separate from the gaslight. The first gas-lamps burned in the arcades. The attempt to use them under the open sky was made in Baudelaire's childhood; candelabra were placed on the Place Vendôme. Under Napoleon III the number of gas lanterns in Paris increased rapidly.[29] This increased safety in the city made the crowds feel at home in the open streets even at night, and removed the starry sky from the ambience of the big city more reliably than this was done by its tall buildings. 'I draw the curtain behind the sun; now it has been put to bed, as is proper; henceforth I shall see no other light but that of the gas flame.'[30] The moon and the stars are no longer worth mentioning.

In the heyday of the Second Empire, the shops in the main streets did not close before ten o'clock at night. It was the great period of *noctambulisme*. In the chapter of his *Heures parisiennes* which is devoted to the second hour after midnight, Delvau wrote: 'A person may take a rest from time to time; he is permitted stops and resting places; but he has no right to sleep.'[31] On the Lake of Geneva, Dickens nostalgically remembered Genoa where he had two miles of streets by whose light he had been able to roam about at night. Later, when the disappearance of the arcades made stroll-

vol. 1, pp. 621ff. [*The Letters of Charles Dickens*, edited by Walter Dexter, vol. 1: 1832–1846, London, 1938, p. 782.]

28. II, 710.

29. cf. *La transformation de Paris sous le Second Empire. Exposition de la Bibliothèque et des travaux historiques de la ville de Paris*, edited by Marcel Poëte, E. Clouzot and G. Henriot, Paris, 1910, p. 65.

30. Julien Lemer, *Paris au gaz*, Paris, 1861, p. 10. The same image may be found in 'Crépuscule du soir': the sky slowly closes like a big alcove (cf. I, 108.)

31. Alfred Delvau, *Les heures parisiennes*, Paris, 1866, p. 206.

ing go out of style and gaslight was no longer considered fashionable, it seemed to a last *flâneur* who sadly strolled through the
empty Colbert Arcade that the flickering of the gas-lamps indicated
only the fear of the flame that it would not be paid at the end of the
month.[32] That is when Stevenson wrote his plaint about the disappearance of the gas lanterns. He muses particularly on the
rhythm with which lamplighters go through the streets and light
one lantern after another. At first this rhythm contrasted with the
uniformity of the dusk, but now the contrast is with a brutal shock
caused by the spectacle of entire cities suddenly being illuminated
by electric light. 'Such a light as this should shine only on murders
and public crime, or along the corridors of lunatic asylums, a horror
to heighten horror.'[33] There is some indication that only latterly was
such an idyllic view of gaslight taken as Stevenson's, who wrote its
obituary. The above-mentioned story by Poe is a good case in
point. There can hardly be a weirder description of this light: 'The
rays of the gas-lamps, feeble at first in their struggle with the dying
day, had now at length gained ascendancy, and threw over every
thing a fitful and garish lustre. All was dark yet splendid – as that
ebony to which has been likened the style of Tertullian.'[34] 'Inside

32. cf. Louis Veuillot, *Les odeurs de Paris*, Paris, 1914, p. 182.

33. Robert Louis Stevenson, 'A Plea for Gas Lamps', in *Virginibus Puerisque
and Other Papers. Works*, Tusitala Edition, vol. 25, London, 1924, p. 132.

34. There is a parallel to this passage in 'Un Jour de pluie'. Even though this
poem bears another man's name, it may be ascribed to Baudelaire (cf. Charles
Baudelaire, *Vers retrouvés*, edited by Julius Mouquet, Paris, 1929). The
analogy between the last stanza and Poe's mention of Tertullian is all the more
remarkable because the poem was written in 1843 at the latest, at a time when
Baudelaire did not know Poe.

> Chacun, nous coudoyant sur le trottoir glissant,
> Egoiste et brutal, passe et nous éclabousse,
> Ou, pour courir plus vite, en s'éloignant nous pousse.
> Partout fange, déluge, obscurité du ciel:
> Noir tableau qu'eût rêvé le noir Ezéchiel!   (I, 211.)

> (Each one, elbowing us upon the slippery sidewalk, selfish and
> savage, goes by and splashes us, or to run the faster, gives us a
> push as he makes off. Mud everywhere, deluge, darkness in the
> sky. A sombre scene that Ezekiel the sombre might have
> dreamed.)

a house,' wrote Poe elsewhere, 'gas is definitely inadmissible. Its flickering, harsh light offends the eye.'

The London crowd seems as gloomy and confused as the light in which it moves. This is true not only of the rabble that crawls 'out of its dens' at night. The employees of higher rank are described by Poe as follows: 'They had all slightly bald heads, from which the right ears, long used to pen-holding, had an odd habit of standing off on end. I observed that they always removed or settled their hats with both hands, and wore watches, with short gold chains of a substantial and ancient pattern.' In his description Poe did not aim at any direct observation. The uniformities to which the petty bourgeoisie are subjected by virtue of being part of the crowd are exaggerated; their appearance is not far from being uniform. Even more astonishing is the description of the way the crowd moves. 'By far the greater number of those who went by had a satisfied business-like demeanour, and seemed to be thinking only of making their way through the press. Their brows were knit, and their eyes rolled quickly; when pushed against by fellow-wayfarers they evinced no symptom of impatience, but adjusted their clothes and hurried on. Others, still a numerous class, were restless in their movements, had flushed faces, and talked and gesticulated to themselves, as if feeling in solitude on account of the very denseness of the company around. When impeded in their progress, these people suddenly ceased muttering, but redoubled their gesticulations, and awaited, with an absent and overdone smile upon the lips, the course of the persons impeding them. If jostled, they bowed profusely to the jostlers, and appeared overwhelmed with confusion.' One might think he was speaking of half-drunken wretches. Actually, they were 'noblemen, merchants, attorneys, tradesmen, stock-jobbers'. Something other than a psychology of the classes is involved here.[35]

35. The image of America which Marx had seems to be of the same stuff as Poe's description. He emphasizes the 'feverishly youthful pace of material production' in the States and blames this very pace for the fact that there was 'neither time nor opportunity . . . to abolish the old spirit world' (Marx, *Der achtzehnte Brumaire des Louis Bonaparte*, op. cit., p. 30). In Poe there is something demonic even about the physiognomy of the businessmen. Baudelaire describes how as darkness descends 'the harmful demons' awaken in the air 'sluggish as a bunch of businessmen' (I, 108). This passage in 'Le Crépuscule du soir' may have been inspired by Poe's text.

There is a lithograph by Senefelder which represents a gambling club. Not one of those depicted is pursuing the game in the customary fashion. Each man is dominated by an emotion: one shows unrestrained joy; another, distrust of his partner; a third, dull despair; a fourth evinces belligerence; another is getting ready to depart from the world. In its extravagance this lithograph is reminiscent of Poe. Poe's subject, to be sure, is greater, and his means are in keeping with this. His masterly stroke in this description is that he does not show the hopeless isolation of men in their private interests through the variety of their behaviour, as does Senefelder, but expresses this isolation in absurd uniformities of dress or conduct. The servility with which those pushed even go on to apologize, shows where the devices which Poe employs here come from. They are from the repertoire of clowns, and Poe uses them in a fashion similar to that later employed by clowns. In the performance of a clown, there is an obvious reference to economy. With his abrupt movements he imitates both the machines which push the material and the economic boom which pushes the merchandise. The segments of the crowd described by Poe effect a similar mimicry of the 'feverish . . . pace of material production' along with the business forms that go with it. What the fun fair, which turned the little man into a clown, later accomplished with its dodgem cars and related amusements is anticipated in Poe's description. The people in his story behave as if they could no longer express themselves through anything but a reflex action. These goings-on seem even more dehumanized because Poe talks only about people. If the crowd is jammed up, it is not because it is being impeded by vehicular traffic – there is no mention of it anywhere – but because it is being blocked by other crowds. In a mass of this nature the art of strolling could not flourish.

In Baudelaire's Paris things had not come to such a pass. Ferries were still crossing the Seine at points where later there would be bridges. In the year of Baudelaire's death it was still possible for an entrepreneur to cater to the comfort of the well-to-do with a fleet of five hundred sedan chairs circulating about the city. Arcades where the *flâneur* would not be exposed to the sight of carriages that did not recognize pedestrians as rivals were enjoying undiminished popularity. There was the pedestrian who wedged himself into the crowd, but there was also the *flâneur* who demanded elbow room and was unwilling to forego the life of a gentleman of leisure. His leisurely appearance as a personality is his protest against the division of labour which makes people into specialists. It is also his protest against their industriousness. Around 1840 it was briefly fashionable to take turtles for a walk in the arcades. The *flâneurs* liked to have the turtles set the pace for them. If they had had their way, progress would have been obliged to accommodate itself to this pace. But this attitude did not prevail; Taylor, who popularized the watchword 'Down with dawdling!' carried the day.[36] Some people sought to anticipate coming developments while there was still time. Rattier wrote in 1857 in his utopia, *Paris n'existe plus*: 'The *flâneur* whom we used to encounter on the sidewalks and in front of the shop-windows, this nonentity, this constant rubberneck, this inconsequential type who was always in search of cheap emotions and knew about nothing but cobblestones, fiacres, and gas lanterns . . . has now become a farmer, a vintner, a linen manufacturer, a sugar refiner, and a steel magnate.'[37]

On his peregrinations the man of the crowd lands at a late hour in a department store where there still are many customers. He moves about like someone who knows his way around the place. Were there multi-storied department stores in Poe's day? No matter; Poe lets the restless man spend an 'hour and a half, or thereabouts' in this bazaar. 'He entered shop after shop, priced nothing, spoke no word, and looked at all objects with a wild and vacant stare.' If the arcade is the classical form of the *intérieur*, which is how the *flâneur* sees the street, the department store is the form of the *intérieur*'s decay. The bazaar is the last hangout of the *flâneur*. If in the beginning the street had become an *intérieur* for him, now this *intérieur* turned into a street, and he roamed through the labyrinth of merchandise as he had once roamed through the labyrinth of the city. It is a magnificent touch in Poe's story that it includes along with the earliest description of the *flâneur* the figuration of his end.

Jules Laforgue said about Baudelaire that he was the first to speak

36. cf. Georges Friedmann, *La crise du progrès*, Paris, 1936, p. 76.
37. Paul Ernest de Rattier, *Paris n'existe plus*, Paris, 1857, pp. 74ff.

of Paris 'as someone condemned to live in the capital day after day.'[38] He might have said that he was the first to speak also of the opiate that was available to give relief to men so condemned, and only to them. The crowd is not only the newest asylum of outlaws; it is also the latest narcotic for those abandoned. The *flâneur* is someone abandoned in the crowd. In this he shares the situation of the commodity. He is not aware of this special situation, but this does not diminish its effect on him and it permeates him blissfully like a narcotic that can compensate him for many humiliations. The intoxication to which the *flâneur* surrenders is the intoxication of the commodity around which surges the stream of customers.

If the soul of the commodity which Marx occasionally mentions in jest existed,[39] it would be the most empathetic ever encountered in the realm of souls, for it would have to see in everyone the buyer in whose hand and house it wants to nestle. Empathy is the nature of the intoxication to which the *flâneur* abandons himself in the crowd. 'The poet enjoys the incomparable privilege of being himself and someone else as he sees fit. Like a roving soul in search of a body, he enters another person whenever he wishes. For him alone, all is open; if certain places seem closed to him, it is because in his view they are not worth inspecting.'[40] The commodity itself is the speaker here. Yes, the last words give a rather accurate idea of what the commodity whispers to a poor wretch who passes a shop-window containing beautiful and expensive things. These objects are not interested in this person; they do not empathize with him. In the sentences of the significant prose poem 'Les Foules' there speaks, with other words, the fetish itself with which Baudelaire's sensitive nature resonated so powerfully; that empathy with inorganic things which was one of his sources of inspiration.[41]

38. Jules Laforgue, *Mélanges posthumes*, Paris, 1903, p. 111.

39. cf. Marx, *Das Kapital*, edited by Karl Korsch, Berlin, 1932, p. 95 [English edition, op. cit., p. 84].

40. I, 420ff.

41. The second 'Spleen' poem is the most important addition to the documentation for this that was assembled in the first part of this essay. Hardly any poet before Baudelaire wrote a verse that is anything like 'Je suis un vieux boudoir plein de roses fanées' (I, 86) ('I am an old boudoir full of faded roses'). The poem is entirely based on empathy with material that is dead in a

Baudelaire was a connoisseur of narcotics, yet one of their most important social effects probably escaped him. It consists in the charm displayed by addicts under the influence of drugs. Commodities derive the same effect from the crowd that surges around and intoxicates them. The concentration of customers which makes the market, which in turn makes the commodity into a commodity, enhances its attractiveness to the average buyer. When Baudelaire speaks of 'the big cities' state of religious intoxication',[42] the commodity is probably the unnamed subject of this state. And the 'holy prostitution of the soul' compared with which 'that which people call love is quite small, quite limited, and quite feeble'[43] really can be nothing else than the prostitution of the commodity-soul – if the confrontation with love retains its meaning. Baudelaire refers to 'that holy prostitution of the soul which gives itself wholly, poetry and charity, to the unexpected that appears, to the unknown that passes' ('*cette sainte prostitution de l'âme qui se donne tout entière, poésie et charité, à l'imprévu qui se montre, à l'inconnu qui passe*').[44] It is this very *poésie* and this very *charité* which the prostitutes claim for themselves. They had tried the secrets of the open markets; in this respect commodities had no advantage over them. Some of

---

dual sense. It is inorganic matter, matter that has been eliminated from the circulation process.

> Désormais tu n'es plus, ô matière vivante!
> Qu'un granit entouré d'une vague épouvante,
> Assoupi dans le fond d'un Sahara brumeux;
> Un vieux sphinx ignoré du monde insoucieux,
> Oublié sur la carte, et dont l'humeur farouche
> Ne chante qu'aux rayons du soleil qui se couche (I, 86).

(Henceforth, O living matter, you are nothing more
Than the fixed heart of chaos, soft horror's granite core,
Than a forgotten Sphinx that in some desert stands,
Drowsing beneath the heat, half-hidden by the sands,
Unmarked on any map, – whose rude and sullen frown
Lights up a moment only when the sun goes down.)

translated by Edna St Vincent Millay

The image of the Sphinx which concludes the poem has the gloomy beauty of unsaleable articles such as may still be found in arcades.

42. II, 627.   43. I, 421.   44. I, 421.

the commodity's charms were based on the market, and they turned into as many means of power. As such they were registered by Baudelaire in his 'Crépuscule du soir':

> A travers les lueurs que tourmente le vent
> La Prostitution s'allume dans les rues;
> Comme une fourmilière elle ouvre ses issues;
> Partout elle se fraye un occulte chemin,
> Ainsi que l'ennemi qui tente un coup de main;
> Elle remue au sein de la cité de fange
> Comme un ver qui dérobe à l'Homme ce qu'il mange.[45]

> (Against the lamplight, whose shivering is the wind's,
> Prostitution spreads its light and life in the streets:
> Like an anthill opening its issue it penetrates
> Mysteriously everywhere by its own occult route;
> Like an enemy mining the foundations of a fort,
> Or a worm in an apple, eating what all should eat,
> It circulates securely in the city's clogged heart.)

translated by David Paul

Only the mass of inhabitants permits prostitution to spread over large parts of the city. And only the mass makes it possible for the sexual object to become intoxicated with the hundred stimuli which it produces.

Not everyone found the spectacle offered by the people in the streets of a big city intoxicating. Long before Baudelaire wrote his prose poem 'Les Foules', Friedrich Engels had undertaken to describe the bustle in the streets of London. 'A town such as London, where a man might wander for hours together without reaching the beginning of the end, without meeting the slightest hint which could lead to the inference that there is open country within reach, is a strange thing. This colossal centralization, this heaping together of two and a half millions of human beings at one point, has multiplied the power of this two and a half millions a hundredfold. . . . But the sacrifices which all this has cost become apparent later. After roaming the streets of the capital a day or two, making headway with difficulty through the human turmoil and the

45. I, 108.

endless lines of vehicles, after visiting the slums of the metropolis, one realizes for the first time that these Londoners have been forced to sacrifice the best qualities of their human nature, to bring to pass all the marvels of civilization which crowd their city. . . . The very turmoil of the streets has something repulsive, something against which human nature rebels. The hundreds of thousands of all classes and ranks crowding past each other, are they not all human beings with the same qualities and powers, and with the same interest in being happy? . . . And still they crowd by one another as though they had nothing in common, nothing to do with one another, and their only agreement is the tacit one, that each keep to his own side of the pavement, so as not to delay the opposing stream of the crowd, while it occurs to no man to honour another with so much as a glance. The brutal indifference, the unfeeling isolation of each in his private interest, becomes the more repellent and offensive, the more these individuals are crowded together, within a limited space.'⁴⁶

The *flâneur* only seems to break through this 'unfeeling isolation of each in his private interest' by filling the hollow space created in him by such isolation, with the borrowed – and fictitious – isolations of strangers. Next to Engels's clear description, it sounds obscure when Baudelaire writes: 'The pleasure of being in a crowd is a mysterious expression of the enjoyment of the multiplication of numbers.'⁴⁷ But this statement becomes clear if one imagines it spoken not only from a person's viewpoint but also from the viewpoint of a commodity. To be sure, insofar as a person, as labour power, is a commodity, there is no need for him to identify himself as such. The more conscious he becomes of his mode of existence, the mode imposed upon him by the system of production, the more he proletarianizes himself, the more he will be gripped by the chill of the commodity economy and the less he will feel like empathizing with commodities. But things had not reached that point with the class of the petty bourgeoisie to which Baudelaire belonged. On the scale with which we are dealing here, this class was only at the

46. Engels, *Die Lage der arbeitenden Klasse in England*, Leipzig, 1848, pp. 36ff. [Original (1887) English translation, *The Condition of the Working-Class in England in 1844*, in Karl Marx and Friedrich Engels, *On Britain*, Moscow, 1962, pp. 56–7.]   47. II, 626.

beginning of its decline. Inevitably, one day many of its members had to become aware of the commodity nature of their labour power. But this day had not as yet come; until that day they were permitted, if one may put it that way, to pass their time. The very fact that their share could at best be enjoyment, but never power, made the period which history gave them a space for passing time. Anyone who sets out to while away time seeks enjoyment. It was self-evident, however, that the more this class wanted to have its enjoyment *in* this society, the more limited this enjoyment would be. The enjoyment promised to be less limited if this class found enjoyment *of* this society possible. If it wanted to achieve virtuosity in this kind of enjoyment, it could not spurn empathizing with commodities. It had to enjoy this identification with all the pleasure and the uneasiness which derived from a presentiment of its own destiny as a class. Finally, it had to approach this destiny with a sensitivity that perceives charm even in damaged and decaying goods. Baudelaire, who in a poem to a courtesan called her heart 'bruised like a peach, ripe like her body, for the lore of love', possessed this sensitivity. To it he owed his enjoyment of this society as someone who had already half withdrawn from it.

In the attitude of someone with this kind of enjoyment he let the spectacle of the crowd act upon him. The deepest fascination of this spectacle lay in the fact that as it intoxicated him it did not blind him to the horrible social reality. He remained conscious of it, though only in the way in which intoxicated people are 'still' aware of reality. That is why in Baudelaire the big city almost never finds expression in the direct presentation of its inhabitants. The directness and harshness with which Shelley captured London through the depiction of its people could not benefit Baudelaire's Paris.

> Hell is a city much like London,
> A populous and a smoky city;
> There are all sorts of people undone,
> And there is little or no fun done;
> Small justice shown, and still less pity.[48]

48. Percy Bysshe Shelley, 'Peter Bell the Third Part', *Complete Poetical Works*, London, 1932, p. 346. [Benjamin quoted this verse in a German version by Bertolt Brecht.]

For the *flâneur* there is a veil over this picture. This veil is the mass; it billows in 'the twisting folds of the old metropolises'.[49] Because of it, horrors have an enchanting effect upon him.[50] Only when this veil tears and reveals to the *flâneur* 'one of the populous squares . . . which are empty during street fighting'[51] does he, too, get an unobstructed view of the big city.

If any proof were needed of the force with which the experience of the crowd moved Baudelaire, it would be the fact that he undertook to vie with Hugo in this experience. That Hugo's strength lay here, if anywhere, was evident to Baudelaire. He praises a '*caractère poétique . . . interrogatif*'[52] in Hugo and says that Hugo not only knows how to reproduce clear things sharply and distinctly but also reproduces with the requisite obscurity what has manifested itself only dimly and indistinctly. One of the three poems of the *Tableaux parisiens* which are dedicated to Hugo begins with an invocation of the crowded city: 'Teeming city, city full of dreams.'[53] Another follows old women in the 'teeming tableau'[54] of the city, right through the crowd.[55] The crowd is a new subject in lyric poetry. Of the innovator Sainte-Beuve it was said appreciatively, as something fitting and appropriate for a poet, that 'the crowd was unbearable'[56] for him. During his exile in Jersey, Hugo opened this subject up for poetry. On his walks along the coast, this subject took shape for him, thanks to one of the enormous antitheses that were indispensable to his inspiration. In Hugo the crowd enters literature as an object of contemplation. The surging ocean is its model, and the thinker who reflects on this eternal spectacle is the true explorer of the crowd in which he loses himself as he loses himself in the roaring of the sea. 'As the exile on his lonely cliff looks out towards the great, fateful countries, he looks down into the past of the peoples. . . . He carries himself and his destiny into the fullness of events;

49. I, 102   50. cf. I, 102.   51. II, 193.
52. II, 522.   53. I, 100.   54. I, 103.
55. The third poem of the cycle, 'Les Petites vieilles', underlines the rivalry by following the third poem in Hugo's cycle, *Fantômes*, verbatim. Thus there is a correspondence between one of Baudelaire's most perfect poems and one of Hugo's weakest.
56. Sainte-Beuve, *Les consolations. Pensées d'août*, Paris, 1863, p. 125. (The remark, published by Sainte-Beuve from the manuscript, is by Farcy.)

they become alive in him and blend with the life of the natural forces – with the sea, the crumbling rocks, the shifting clouds, and the other exalted things that are part of a lonely, quiet life in communion with nature.'[57] 'The ocean itself got bored with him' (*'L'océan même s'est ennuyé de lui'*), said Baudelaire about Hugo, touching the man brooding on the cliffs with the light-pencil of his irony. Baudelaire did not feel inclined to follow the spectacle of nature. His experience of the crowd bore the traces of the 'heart-ache and the thousand natural shocks' which a pedestrian suffers in the bustle of a city and which keep his self-awareness all the more alert. (Basically it is this very self-awareness that he lends to the strolling commodity.) To Baudelaire the crowd never was a stimulus to cast the plummet of his thought down into the depths of the world. Hugo, on the other hand, writes, 'The depths are crowds' (*'Les profondeurs sont des multitudes'*),[58] and thereby gives an enormous scope to his thinking. The natural-supernatural which affected Hugo in the form of the crowd presents itself in the forest, in the animal kingdom, and by the surging sea; in any of those places the physiognomy of a big city can flash for a few moments. 'La Pente de la rêverie' gives a splendid idea of the promiscuity at work among the multitude of living things.

> La nuit avec la foule, en ce rêve hideux,
> Venait d'épaississant ensemble toutes deux,
> Et, dans ces regions que nul regard ne sonde,
> Plus l'homme était nombreux,
>   plus l'ombre était profonde.[59]

> (In that hideous dream, night arrived together with the crowd, and both grew ever thicker; indeed, in those regions which no look can fathom, the more numerous were the people, the deeper was the darkness.)

57. Hugo von Hofmannsthal, *Versuch über Victor Hugo*, Munich, 1925, p. 49.

58. Quoted in Gabriel Bounoure, 'Abîmes de Victor Hugo', in *Mesures*, 15 July 1936, p. 39.

59. Victor Hugo, *Oeuvres complètes. Édition définitive. Poésie II: Les Orientales, Les Feuilles d'automne*, Paris, 1880, pp. 365ff.

And:

> Foule sans nom! chaos! des voix, des yeux, des pas.
> Ceux qu'on n'a jamais vu, ceux qu'on ne connaît pas.
> Tous les vivants! – cités bourdonnantes aux oreilles
> Plus qu'un bois d'Amérique ou une ruche d'abeilles.[60]

> (Nameless mob! chaos! voices, eyes, steps. Those one has never seen, those no one knows. All the living! – cities buzzing in our ears louder than an American forest or a beehive.)

With the crowd, nature exercises its fundamental right on the city. But it is not nature alone which exercises its rights in this way. There is an astonishing place in *Les Misérables* where what goes on in the forest appears as the archetype of mass existence. 'What had happened on this street would not have astonished a forest. The tree trunks and the underbrush, the herbs, the inextricably inter-twined branches, and the tall grasses lead an obscure kind of existence. Invisible things flit through the teeming immensity. What is below human beings perceives through a fog that which is above them.'[61] This description contains the characteristics of Hugo's experience with the crowd. In the crowd that which is below a person comes in contact with what holds sway above him. It is this promiscuity that includes all others. In Hugo the crowd appears as a bastard which shapeless, superhuman powers create from those below human beings. In the visionary strain that is con-tained in Hugo's conception of the crowd, social reality gets its due more than it does in the 'realistic' treatment which he gave the crowd in politics. For the crowd really is a spectacle of nature – if one may apply the term to social conditions. A street, a conflagra-tion, or a traffic accident assemble people who are not defined along class lines. They present themselves as concrete gatherings, but socially they remain abstract – namely, in their isolated private interests. Their models are the customers who, each in his private interest, gather at the market around their 'common cause'. In many cases, such gatherings have only a statistical existence. This exist-

60. ibid., p. 363.
61. Hugo, op. cit., Roman VIII, *Les Misérables*, Paris, 1881.

ence conceals the really monstrous thing about them: the concentration of private persons as such by the accident of their private interests. But if these concentrations become evident – and the totalitarian states see to it by making the concentration of their clients permanent and obligatory for all their purposes – their hybrid character clearly manifests itself, and particularly to those who are involved. They rationalize the accident of the market economy which brings them together in this way as 'fate' in which 'the race' gets together again. In doing so they give free rein to both the herd instinct and to reflective action. The peoples who are in the foreground of the Western European stage make the acquaintance of the supernatural which confronted Hugo in the crowd. Hugo, to be sure, was not able to assess the historical significance of this force. However, it left its imprint on his work as a strange distortion, in the form of spiritualistic protocols.

Hugo's contact with the spirit world which, as we know, had an equally profound effect on his life and his production in Jersey, was, strange though this may seem, primarily a contact with the masses which the poet necessarily missed in exile. For the crowd is the spirit world's mode of existence. Thus Hugo saw himself primarily as a genius in a great assembly of geniuses who were his ancestors. In his *William Shakespeare*, he devoted one rhapsodic page after another to the procession of those aristocrats of the intellect, beginning with Moses and ending with Hugo. But they constitute only a small group in the tremendous multitude of the departed. To Hugo's chthonian mind, the *ad plures ire* [dying] of the Romans was not an empty phrase.

The spirits of the dead came late, as messengers of the night, in the last séance. Hugo's Jersey notes have preserved their messages: 'Every great man works on two works – the work he creates as a living person and his spirit-work. A living man devotes himself to the first work. But in the deep still of night the spirit-creator – oh horror! – awakens in him. What?! – cries the person – isn't that all? No, replies the spirit; arise. The storm is raging, dogs and foxes are howling, darkness is everywhere, nature shudders and winces under the whip of God. . . . The spirit-creator sees the phantom idea. The words bristle and the sentence shudders . . . the windowpanes get fogged and dull, the lamp is seized by fright. . . . Watch out, living person, man of a century, you vassal of an idea that comes from the earth. For this is madness, this is the grave, this is infinity, this is a phantom idea.'[62] The cosmic shudder during the experience of the invisible which Hugo preserves here has no similarity to the naked terror which overcame Baudelaire in the *spleen*. Also, Baudelaire mustered only little understanding for Hugo's undertaking. 'True civilization,' he said, 'does not lie in table-turning at séances.' But Hugo was not concerned with civilization. He felt truly at home in the spirit world. One could say that it was the cosmic complement of a household of which horror was an integral part. His intimate acquaintance with the apparitions removes much of their frightening quality. It is not without fussiness and brings out the threadbare nature of the apparitions. As pendants to the nocturnal ghosts there are meaningless abstractions, more or less ingenious embodiments that may be found on the monuments of the time. In the Jersey protocols, 'Drama', 'Poetry', 'Literature', 'Thought', and many things of that type may freely be heard next to the voices of chaos.

For Hugo the immense throngs of the spirit world are – and this may bring the riddle closer to a solution – primarily a public. It is less strange that his work absorbed motifs of the talking table than that he customarily produced it in front of the table. The acclaim which the beyond gave him unstintingly while he was in exile gave him a foretaste of the immeasurable acclaim which was to await him at home in his old age. When on his seventieth birthday the population of the capital pressed toward his house on Avenue d'Eylau, this meant the realization of the image of the wave surging against the cliffs as well as the realization of the message of the spirit world.

In the final analysis, the impenetrable obscurity of mass existence was also the source of Victor Hugo's revolutionary speculations. In the *Châtiments* the day of liberation is circumscribed as

> Le jour où nos pillards, où nos tyrans sans nombre
> Comprendront que quelqu'un remue au fond de l'ombre.[63]

(The day on which our pillagers, our tyrants without

62. Gustave Simon, *Chez Victor Hugo. Les tables tournantes de Jersey*, Paris, 1923, pp. 306ff.

63. Hugo, op. cit., *Poésie IV: Les Châtiments*, Paris, 1882 ('La Caravane IV').

number, will understand that there is someone stirring
deep in the darkness.)

Could there be a reliable revolutionary judgment in keeping with
this view, based on the crowd, of the suppressed masses? Was not
this view, rather, clear evidence of the limitation of this judgment,
no matter what its origin? In the Chamber debate of 25 November
1848, Hugo had inveighed against Cavaignac's barbaric suppression
of the June revolt. But on 20 June, in the discussion of the *ateliers
nationaux*, he said: 'The monarchy had its idlers, the republic has its
loafers.'[64] Hugo reflected the superficial views of the day as well as
a blind faith in the future, but he also had a profound vision of the
life that was forming in the womb of nature and of the people.
Hugo never succeeded in fashioning a bridge between these two.
He saw no need for such a bridge, and this explains the tremendous
pretensions and scope of his work and presumably also the tremendous influence of his life-work on his contemporaries. In the
chapter of *Les Misérables* which is entitled 'L'argot', the two con-
flicting sides of his nature confront each other with impressive
harshness. After a bold look into the linguistic workshop of the
lower classes, the poet concludes by writing: 'Since 1789 the whole
people has unfolded in the purified individual. There is no poor
man who does not have his rights and thus the light that falls upon
him. A poor wretch bears the honour of France inside him. The
dignity of a citizen is an inner bulwark. Anyone who is free is
conscientious; and everyone who has the vote rules.'[65] Victor Hugo
saw things the way the experiences of a successful literary and

64. Pélin, a characteristic representative of the lower *bohème*, wrote about
this speech in his paper *Les boulets rouges. Feuille du club pacifique des droits
de l'homme*: 'The *citoyen* Hugo has made his début in the National Assembly.
As had been expected, he turned out to be a declaimer, a gesticulator, and a
phrase-monger. In the vein of his latest crafty and defamatory poster he spoke
of the idlers, the poor, the loafers, the *lazzaroni*, the praetorians of the revolution, and the *condottieri* – in a word, he wore out metaphors and ended with
an attack on the *ateliers nationaux*' (*Les boulets rouges*, First year, June 22–24).
In his *Histoire parlementaire de la Seconde République*, Eugène Spuller writes:
'Victor Hugo had been elected with reactionary votes. . . . He had always
voted with the Rightists, except for one or two occasions in which politics
did not matter' (Paris, 1891, pp. 111 and 266).

65. Hugo, op. cit., *Les Misérables*, p. 306.

political career presented them to him. He was the first great writer whose works have collective titles: *Les Misérables, Les Travailleurs de la mer*. To him the crowd meant, almost in the ancient sense, the crowd of clients – that is, the masses of his readers and his voters. Hugo was, in a word, no *flâneur*.

For the crowd which went with Hugo and with which he went there was no Baudelaire. But this crowd did exist for Baudelaire. Seeing it caused him every day to plumb the depth of his failure, and this probably was not the least among the reasons why he sought this sight. The desperate pride which thus befell him – in bursts, as it were – was fed by the fame of Victor Hugo. But he was probably spurred on even more strongly by Hugo's political creed, the creed of the *citoyen*. The masses of the big city could not disconcert him. He recognized the crowd of people in them and wanted to be flesh of their flesh. Laicism, Progress, and Democracy were inscribed on the banner which he waved over their heads. This banner transfigured mass existence. It shaded a threshold which separated the individual from the crowd. Baudelaire guarded this threshold, and that differentiated him from Victor Hugo. However, he resembled him in that he, too, did not see through the social aura which is crystallized in the crowd. He therefore opposed to it a model which was as uncritical as Hugo's conception of the crowd. This model was the hero. When Victor Hugo was celebrating the crowd as the hero in a modern epic, Baudelaire was looking for a refuge for the hero among the masses of the big city. Hugo placed himself in the crowd as a *citoyen*; Baudelaire sundered himself from it as a hero.

III. Modernism

Baudelaire patterned his image of the artist after an image of the hero. From the beginning, each is an advocate of the other. In the 'Salon de 1845' he wrote: 'Will-power has to be well developed, and always very fruitful, to be able to give the stamp of uniqueness even to second-rate works. The viewer enjoys the effort and his eye drinks the sweat.'[1] In the *Conseils aux jeunes littérateurs* of the following year there is a fine formula in which the *'contemplation opiniâtre de l'oeuvre de demain'*[2] appears as the guarantee of inspiration. Baudelaire knows the *'indolence naturelle des inspirés'*;[3] Musset – so he says – never understood how much work it takes 'to let a work of art emerge from a daydream'.[4] He, on the other hand, comes before the public from the very first moment with his own code, precepts, and taboos. Barrès claimed that he could recognize 'in every little word of Baudelaire a trace of the toil that helped him achieve such great things'.[5] 'Even in his nervous crises,' writes Gourmont, 'Baudelaire retains something healthy.'[6] The most felicitous formulation is given by the symbolist Gustave Kahn when he says that 'with Baudelaire, poetic work resembled a physical effort'.[7] Proof of this may be found in his work – in a metaphor worth closer inspection.

1. II, 26.   2. II, 388.   3. II, 531.
4. Albert Thibaudet, *Intérieurs*, Paris, 1924, p. 15.
5. Quoted in André Gide, 'Baudelaire et M. Faguet', in *Nouvelle revue française*, 1 November 1910, p. 513.
6. Rémy de Gourmont, *Promenades littéraires. Deuxième série*, Paris, 1906, pp. 85ff.
7. Preface by Gustave Kahn in Baudelaire, *Mon coeur mis à nu et Fusées*, Paris, 1909, p. 6.

It is the metaphor of the fencer. Baudelaire was fond of using it to present martial elements as artistic elements. When he describes Constantin Guys, to whom he was attached, he catches him at a time when others are asleep. How he stands there 'bent over his table, scrutinizing the sheet of paper just as intently as he does the objects around him by day; how he *stabs away* with his pencil, his pen, his brush, spurts water from his glass to the ceiling and tries his pen on his shirt; how he pursues his work swiftly and intensely, as though afraid that his images might escape him; thus he is combative, even when alone, and parries his own blows'.[8] In the opening stanza of his poem 'Le Soleil', Baudelaire portrayed himself in the throes of such 'curious exercise', and this is probably the only place in the *Fleurs du mal* where he is shown at his poetic labours. The duel in which every artist is engaged and in which he 'screams with fright before he is vanquished'[9] is given the framework of an idyll; its violence recedes into the background and its charm may be recognized.

> Le long du vieux faubourg, où pendent aux masures
> Les persiennes, abri des secrètes luxures,
> Quand le soleil cruel frappe à traits redoublés
> Sur la ville et les champs, sur les toits et les blés,
> Je vais m'exercer seul à ma fantasque escrime,
> Flairant dans tous les coins les hasards de la rime,
> Trébuchant sur les mots comme sur les pavés,
> Heurtant parfois des vers depuis longtemps rêvés.[10]

> (Through the old suburb, where the persian blinds hang at the windows of tumbledown houses, hiding furtive pleasures; when the cruel sun strikes blow upon blow on the city and the meadows, the roofs and the cornfields, I go practising my fantastic fencing all alone, scenting a chance rhyme in every corner, stumbling against words as against cobblestones, sometimes striking on verses I had long dreamt of.)

translated by Francis Scarfe

8. II, 334.
9. Quoted in Ernest Raynaud, *Charles Baudelaire*, Paris, 1922, pp. 317ff.
10. I, 96.

To give these prosodic experiences their due in prose as well was one of the intentions which Baudelaire had pursued in the *Spleen de Paris*, his poems in prose. In his dedication of this collection to Arsène Houssaye, the editor-in-chief of *La Presse*, Baudelaire expresses, in addition to this intention, what was really at the bottom of those experiences. 'Who among us has not dreamt, in moments of ambition, of the miracle of a poetic prose, musical without rhythm and without rhyme, supple and staccato enough to adapt to the lyrical stirrings of the soul, the undulations of dreams, and the sudden leaps of consciousness? This obsessive ideal is above all a child of the experience of giant cities, of the intersecting of their myriad relations.'[11]

If one tries to picture this rhythm and investigate this mode of work, it turns out that Baudelaire's *flâneur* was not a self-portrait of the poet to the extent that this might be assumed. An important trait of the real-life Baudelaire – that is, of the man committed to his work – is not part of this portrayal: his absentmindedness. In the *flâneur*, the joy of watching is triumphant. It can concentrate on observation; the result is the amateur detective. Or it can stagnate in the gaper; then the *flâneur* has turned into a *badaud*.[12] The revealing presentations of the big city have come from neither. They are the work of those who have traversed the city absently, as it were, lost in thought or worry. The image of *fantasque escrime* does justice to them; Baudelaire has in mind their condition which is anything but the condition of the observer. In his book on Dickens, Chesterton has masterfully captured the man who roams about the big city lost in thought. Charles Dickens's steady peregrinations had begun in his childhood. 'Whenever he had done drudging, he had no other resource but drifting, and he drifted over half London. He was a dreamy child, thinking mostly of his own dreary prospects.

11. I, 405ff.

12. 'The *flâneur* must not be confused with the *badaud*; a nuance should be observed there. . . . The simple *flâneur* is always in full possession of his individuality, whereas the individuality of the *badaud* disappears. It is absorbed by the outside world . . . which intoxicates him to the point where he forgets himself. Under the influence of the spectacle which presents itself to him, the *badaud* becomes an impersonal creature; he is no longer a human being, he is part of the public, of the crowd' (Victor Fournel, *Ce qu'on voit dans les rues de Paris*, Paris, 1858, p. 263).

. . . He walked in darkness under the lamps of Holborn, and was crucified at Charing Cross. . . . He did not go in for "observation", a priggish habit; he did not look at Charing Cross to improve his mind or count the lamp-posts in Holborn to practise his arithmetic. . . . Dickens did not stamp these places on his mind; he stamped his mind on these places.'[13]

In his later years Baudelaire was not often able to move through the streets of Paris as a stroller. His creditors pursued him, his illness made itself felt, and there was strife between him and his mistress. The shocks which his worries caused him and the hundred ideas with which he parried them were reproduced by Baudelaire the poet in the feints of his prosody. To recognize the labour that Baudelaire bestowed upon his poems under the image of fencing means to learn to comprehend them as a continuous series of tiny improvisations. The variants of his poems indicate how constantly he was at work and how much he was concerned with the least of them. The expeditions on which he bumped into his poetic problem children on the street corners of Paris were not always undertaken voluntarily. In the early years of his life as a littérateur, when he was living at the Hotel Pimodan, his friends had occasion to admire the discretion with which he would remove all traces of work, starting with his desk, from his room.[14] In those days he had, symbolically speaking, set out to capture the streets. Later, when he abandoned one part of his bourgeois existence after another, the street increasingly became a place of refuge for him. But in strolling, there was from the outset an awareness of the fragility of this existence. It makes a virtue out of necessity, and in this it displays the structure

13. G. K. Chesterton, *Dickens*, Paris, 1927, p. 30 [New York, 1906, pp. 45–46].

14. Recalling the period around 1845, Prarond, a friend of Baudelaire's youth, wrote: 'We seldom used writing desks at which to reflect and write.' Referring to Baudelaire he continues: 'I for my part was more likely to see him composing his verses in a hurry, rushing up and down the street; I did not see him sitting before a ream of paper' (quoted in Alphonse Séché, *La vie des Fleurs du mal*, Paris, 1928, p. 84). Banville makes a similar report about the Hotel Pimodan: 'When I got there for the first time I found neither encyclopedias nor a study nor a writing desk. Nor was there a sideboard, a dining room, or anything resembling the furnishings of a middle-class apartment' (Théodore de Banville, *Mes souvenirs*, Paris, 1882, p. 82).

which is in every way characteristic of Baudelaire's conception of the hero.

The necessity which is here disguised is not only a material one; it concerns poetic production. The stereotypes in Baudelaire's experiences, the lack of mediation between his ideas, and the congealed uneasiness in his features indicate that he did not have at his disposal the reserves which great knowledge and a comprehensive view of history give a person. 'Baudelaire had what is a great defect in a writer, a defect of which he was not aware: he was ignorant. What he knew, he knew thoroughly; but he knew little. He remained unacquainted with history, physiology, archaeology, and philosophy. . . . He had little interest in the outside world; he may have been aware of it, but he certainly did not study it.'[15] In the face of this and similar criticisms,[16] it may be natural and legitimate to point to the necessary and useful inaccessibility of a working poet and to the idiosyncratic touches which are essential to all productivity. But there is another side to the situation, and it promotes the overtaxing of the productive person in the name of a principle, the principle of 'creativity'. This overtaxing is all the more dangerous because as it flatters the self-esteem of the productive person, it effectively guards the interests of a social order that is hostile to him. The life-style of the bohemian has contributed to creating a superstition about creativeness which Marx has countered with an observation that applies equally to intellectual and to manual labour. To the opening sentence of the draft of the Gotha programme, 'Labour is the source of all wealth and all culture', he appends this critical note: 'The bourgeois have very good reasons for imputing supernatural creative power to labour, since it follows precisely from the fact that labour depends on nature, that a man who has no other property than his labour must be in all societies and civilizations the slave of other people who have become proprietors of the material working conditions.'[17] Baudelaire owned few of the material conditions of intellectual labour. From a library to an apartment there was nothing that he did not have to do

---

15. Maxime Du Camp, *Souvenirs littéraires*, vol. 2, Paris, 1906, p. 65.

16. cf. Georges Rency, *Physiognomies littéraires*, Brussels, 1907, p. 288.

17. Marx, *Randglossen zum Programm der Deutschen Arbeiterpartei*, edited by Karl Korsch, Berlin, 1922, p. 22.

without in the course of his life, which was equally unsteady in Paris and outside the city. On 26 December 1853, he wrote to his mother: 'I am used to physical suffering to a certain degree. I am adept at making do with two shirts under torn trousers and a jacket which lets in the wind, and I am so experienced in using straw or even paper to plug up the holes in my shoes that moral suffering is almost the only kind I perceive as suffering. However, I must admit that I have reached the point where I don't make any sudden movements or walk a lot because I fear that I might tear my clothes even more.'[18] Among the experiences which Baudelaire has transfigured in the image of the hero, experiences of this kind were the least equivocal.

Around that time, the dispossessed person appears in the shape of the hero in another place and in ironic form: in the writings of Marx. Marx speaks of the ideas of Napoleon I and says: 'The culmination of the "*idées napoléoniennes*" is the preponderance of the army. The army was the *point d'honneur* of farmers working a plot of land who were transformed into heroes.' Now, however, under Napoleon III the army 'no longer is the flower of farm youth, but the swamp flower of the peasant *lumpenproletariat*. It consists largely of *remplaçants* . . . just as the second Bonaparte is himself a *remplaçant*, a substitute for Napoleon.'[19] If one turns away from this view and returns to the image of the fighting poet, one will find another image momentarily superimposed upon it: the image of the marauder, the soldier who roams through the countryside.[20] Above all, however, two famous lines of Baudelaire with their

18. Baudelaire, *Dernières lettres inédites à sa mère*, Crépet, Paris, 1926, pp. 44ff.

19. Marx, *Der achtzehnte Brumaire des Louis Bonaparte*, op. cit., pp. 122ff.

20. cf. '*Pour toi, vieux maraudeur,/L'amour n'a plus de goût, non plus que la dispute*' (I, 89). One of the few repulsive phenomena in the extensive, mostly colourless literature about Baudelaire is the book of one Peter Klassen. It is characteristic of this book, which is written in the distorting terminology of the George circle and, as it were, presents Baudelaire under a steel helmet, that it placed at the centre of his life the ultramontane restoration – that is, the moment 'when in the spirit of the restored divine right of kings the Holy of Holies was carried through the streets of Paris surrounded by shiny arms. This may have been a decisive experience of his entire existence, because it involved his very essence' (Peter Klassen, *Baudelaire*, Weimar, 1931, p. 9). Baudelaire was six years of age at the time.

inconspicuous syncope resound more distinctly over the socially empty space of which Marx speaks. They conclude the second stanza of the third poem of 'Les Petites vieilles'. Proust accompanies them with the words '*il semble impossible d'aller au-delà*' ('it seems impossible to go beyond this').[21]

> Ah! que j'en ai suivi, de ces petites vieilles!
> Une, entre autres, à l'heure où le soleil tombant
> Ensanglante le ciel de blessures vermeilles,
> Pensive, s'asseyait à l'écart sur un banc,
>
> Pour entendre un de ces concerts, riches de cuivre,
> Dont les soldats parfois inondent nos jardins,
> Et qui, dans ces soirs d'or où l'on se sent revivre,
> Versent quelque héroisme au coeur des citadins.[22]
>
> (Yes, I have followed them, time and again!
> One, I recall, when sunset, like a heart,
> Bled through the sky from wounds of ruddy stain,
> Pensively sat upon a seat apart,
>
> To listen to the music, rich in metal,
> That's played by bands of soldiers in the parks
> On golden, soul-reviving eves, to fettle,
> From meek civilian hearts, heroic sparks.)

translated by Roy Campbell

The brass bands staffed by the sons of impoverished peasants which play their melodies for the poor city population – they represent the heroism that shyly hides its threadbare quality in the word *quelque* and is in this very gesture genuine and the only kind that is still produced by this society. In the hearts of its heroes there is no emotion for which there would not be room in the hearts of the little people who gather around a military band.

The parks – the poem refers to them as *nos jardins* – are those open to city-dwellers whose longing is directed in vain at the large,

21. Marcel Proust, 'A propos de Baudelaire', in *Nouvelle revue française*, 1 June 1921, p. 646.

22. I, 104.

closed parks. The people that come to these parks are not entirely the crowd that swirls about the *flâneur*. 'No matter what party one may belong to,' wrote Baudelaire in 1851, 'it is impossible not to be gripped by the spectacle of this sickly population which swallows the dust of the factories, breathes in particles of cotton, and lets its tissues be permeated by white lead, mercury and all the poisons needed for the production of masterpieces'. . .; of this languishing and pining population to whom *the earth owes its wonders*; who feel *a purple and impetuous blood coursing through their veins*, and who cast a long, sorrow-laden look at the sunlight and shadows of the great parks.'[23] This population is the background against which the outlines of the hero stand out. Baudelaire captioned the picture thus presented in his own way. He wrote the words *la modernité* under it.

The hero is the true subject of modernism. In other words, it takes a heroic constitution to live modernism. That was also Balzac's opinion. With their belief, Balzac and Baudelaire are in opposition to Romanticism. They transfigure passions and resolution; the Romanticists transfigured renunciation and surrender. But the new way of looking at things is far more variegated and richer in reservations in a poet than in a storyteller. Two figures of speech will demonstrate how this is so. Both introduce the hero in his modern manifestation to the reader. In Balzac the gladiator becomes a *commis voyageur*. The great travelling salesman Gaudissart is getting ready to work the Touraine. Balzac describes his preparations and interrupts himself to exclaim: 'What an athlete! What an arena! And what weapons: he, the world, and his glib tongue!'[24] Baudelaire on the other hand, recognizes the fencing slave in the proletarian. Of the promises which the wine gives the disinherited, the fifth stanza of the poem 'L'Ame du vin' names the following:

> J'allumerai les yeux de ta femme ravie;
> À ton fils je rendrai sa force et ses couleurs
> Et serai pour ce frêle athlète de la vie
> L'huile qui raffermit les muscles des lutteurs.[25]

23. II, 408.
24. Balzac, *L'illustre Gaudissart*, Calmann-Lévy, Paris, 1892, p. 5.
25. I, 119.

(I'll light the eyes of your enraptured wife;
Give your son strength and make his pale cheeks ruddy
And for this frail athlete of life
Will be the oil that toughens the wrestler's body.)

translated by C. F. MacIntyre

What the man working for wages achieves in his daily work is no less than what in ancient times helped a gladiator win applause and fame. This image is one of the best insights that Baudelaire had; it derives from his reflection about his own situation. A passage from the 'Salon de 1859' indicates how he wanted to have it viewed. 'When I hear how a Raphael or a Veronese are glorified with the veiled intention of depreciating what came after them, . . . I ask myself whether an achievement which must be rated *at least* equal to theirs . . . is not infinitely *more meritorious*, because it triumphed in a hostile atmosphere and place.'[26] Baudelaire was fond of placing his theses in the context crassly, in a baroque illumination, as it were. It was part of his theoretical shrewdness to obscure the connection between them – where one existed. Such obscure passages can almost always be illuminated by his letters. Without having to resort to such a procedure, it is possible to recognize a clear connection between the above passage from 1859 and another passage that was written ten years earlier and is particularly strange. The following chain of reflections will reconstruct this connection.

The resistance which modernism offers to the natural productive élan of a person is out of proportion to his strength. It is understandable if a person grows tired and takes refuge in death. Modernism must be under the sign of suicide, an act which seals a heroic will that makes no concessions to a mentality inimical towards this will. This suicide is not a resignation but a heroic passion. It is *the* achievement of modernism in the realm of passions.[27] In this form, as the *passion particulière de la vie moderne*, suicide appears in the classical passage that is devoted to the theory of modernism. The

26. II, 239.

27. Suicide later was seen by Nietzsche from a similar point of view. 'One cannot condemn Christianity enough, because it devalued the *value* of a . . . great *purging* nihilistic movement which may have been in motion . . . always by opposing the *action of nihilism*, suicide' (Friedrich Nietzsche, *Werke*, edited by Schlechta, Munich, 1956, vol. 3, pp. 792ff.).

suicide of ancient heroes is an exception. 'Apart from Heracles on Mount Oeta, Cato of Utica, and Cleopatra . . . where does one find suicides in the ancient accounts?'[28] Not that Baudelaire could find them in modern accounts; the reference to Rousseau and Balzac which follows this sentence is a meagre one. But modernism does keep the raw material for such presentations in readiness, and it waits for the man who will master it. This raw material has deposited itself in those very strata that have turned out to be the foundation of modernism. The first notes on the theory of modernism were made in 1845. Around that time the idea of suicide became familiar to the working masses. 'People are scrambling for copies of a lithograph depicting an English worker who is taking his life because he despairs of earning a livelihood. One worker even goes to Eugène Sue's apartment and hangs himself there. In his hand there is a slip of paper with this note: "I thought dying would be easier for me if I die under the roof of a man who stands up for us and loves us".'[29] In 1841 Adolphe Boyer, a printer, published a small book entitled *De l'état des ouvriers et de son amélioration par l'organisation du travail*. It was a moderate presentation that sought to recruit the old corporations of itinerant journeymen which stuck to guild practices for the workers' associations. His work was unsuccessful. The author took his own life and in an open letter invited his companions in misfortune to follow suit. Someone like Baudelaire could very well have viewed suicide as the only heroic act that had remained for the *multitudes maladives* of the cities in reactionary times. Perhaps he saw [Alfred] Rethel's 'Death', which he greatly admired, as the work of a subtle artist in front of an easel sketching on a canvas the ways in which suicides died. As regards the colours of the picture, fashion offered its palette.

With the July Monarchy, blacks and greys began to predominate in men's clothes. Baudelaire concerned himself with this innovation in his 'Salon de 1845'. In the conclusion of his first work he wrote: 'More than anyone else, *the* painter, the true painter, will be the man who extracts from present-day life its epic aspects and teaches us in lines and colours to understand how great and poetic we are in our

28. II, 133ff.

29. Charles Benoist, 'L'homme de 1848', in *Revue des deux mondes*, 1 February 1914, p. 667.

patent-leather shoes and our neckties. May the real pioneers next year give us the exquisite pleasure of being allowed to celebrate the advent of the truly *new*.'[30] One year later he wrote: 'Regarding the attire, the covering of the modern hero, . . . does it not have a beauty and a charm of its own? . . . Is this not an attire that is needed by our epoch, suffering, and dressed up to its thin black narrow shoulders in the symbol of constant mourning? The black suit and the frock coat not only have their political beauty as an expression of general equality, but also their poetic beauty as an expression of the public mentality – an immense cortège of undertakers, political undertakers, amorous undertakers, bourgeois undertakers. We all observe some kind of funeral. The unvarying livery of hopelessness is proof of the equality. . . . And haven't the folds in the material, which make grimaces and drape themselves around mortified flesh like snakes, their secret charm?'[31] These mental images are part of the profound fascination which the *femme passante* in mourning of his sonnet exerted upon the poet. The text of 1846 concludes as follows: 'For the heroes of the *Iliad* cannot hold a candle to you, Vautrin, Rastignac, Birotteau – or to you, Fontanarès, who did not dare to confess to the public what you went through under the macabre dress-coat which seems tightened as by a cramp, the dress-coat which all of us wear, or to you, Honoré de Balzac, the strangest, the most romantic, and the most poetic among all the characters created by your imagination.'[32]

Fifteen years later the Southern German Democrat Friedrich Theodor Vischer wrote a critique of men's fashion in which he arrived at insights similar to Baudelaire's. But there is a different emphasis. What provides a hue for the dusky prospectus of modernism in Baudelaire is a shiny argument in the political struggle in Vischer. Contemplating the reaction that had held sway since 1850, Vischer writes: 'To show one's true colours is regarded as ridiculous, to be trim is thought to be childish. Then how could clothes keep from becoming colourless, slack and tight at the same time?'[33] The extremes meet; where it is expressed metaphorically, Vischer's political critique overlaps with an early image of Baudelaire's. In his

30. II, 54ff.   31. II, 134.   32. II, 136.
33. Friedrich Theodor Vischer, *Vernünftige Gedanken über die jetzige Mode. Kritische Gänge*, New Series, Book Three, Stuttgart, 1861, p. 117.

sonnet 'The Albatross' – a product of the overseas trip which, it was hoped, would reform the young poet – Baudelaire recognizes himself in these birds whose awkwardness on the deck where the crew has put them he describes as follows:

> A peine les ont-ils déposés sur les planches,
> Que ces rois de l'azur, maladroits et honteux,
> Laissent piteusement leurs grandes ailes blanches
> Comme des avirons trainer à côté d'eux.
>
> Ce voyageur ailé, comme il est gauche et veule![34]
>
> (Torn from his native space, this captive king
> Flounders upon the deck in stricken pride,
> And pitiably lets his great white wing
> Drag like a heavy paddle at his side.
>
> This rider of winds, how awkward he is, and weak!)

translated by Richard Wilbur

Vischer writes as follows about the wide sleeves of the jacket which cover the wrists: 'Those are not arms any more but rudiments of a wing, stumps of penguin wings and fins of fishes; and the motion of the shapeless appendages when a man walks, looks like foolish, silly gesticulating, shoving, rowing.'[35] The same view of the matter, and the same image.

Not denying the mark of Cain on its brow, Baudelaire more clearly defines the face of modernism as follows: 'The majority of the writers who have concerned themselves with really modern subjects have contented themselves with the certified, official subjects, with our victories and our political heroism. They do this reluctantly and only because the government orders them and pays them for it. And yet there are subjects from private life which are heroic in quite another way. The spectacle of elegant life and of the thousands of irregular existences led in the basements of a big city by criminals and kept women – the *Gazette des Tribunaux* and the *Moniteur* demonstrate that we need only open our eyes to recognize our heroism.'[36] The image of the hero here includes the apache. He

34. I, 22.　　　35. Vischer, op. cit., p. 111.　　　36. II, 134ff.

represents the characteristics which Bounoure sees in Baudelaire's solitude – 'a *noli me tangere*, an enscapsulation of the individual in his difference.'[37] The apache abjures virtue and laws; he terminates the *contrat social* forever. Thus he believes that a world separates him from the bourgeois and fails to recognize in him the features of an accomplice which Hugo was soon to describe with such powerful effect in *Les Châtiments*. Baudelaire's illusions, to be sure, were destined to have far greater staying power. They founded the poetry of apachedom and addressed themselves to a genre which has not disappeared in more than eighty years. Baudelaire was the first to tap this vein. Poe's hero is not the criminal but the detective. Balzac, for his part, knows only the great outsiders of society. Vautrin experiences a rise and a fall; he has a career like all of Balzac's heroes. A criminal career is a career like any other. Ferragus, too, has big ideas and makes long-range plans; he is a Carbonari type. Before Baudelaire, the apache who all his life remained limited to the precincts of society and of the big city, had had no place in literature. The most striking depiction of this subject in the *Fleurs du mal*, 'Le Vin de l'assassin', has become the starting point of a Parisian genre. The cabaret 'Chat noir' became its 'artistic headquarters'. '*Passant, sois moderne*' was the inscription of its early, heroic period.

The poets find the refuse of society on their street and derive their heroic subject from this very refuse. This means that a common type is, as it were, superimposed upon their illustrious type. This new type is permeated by the features of the ragpicker with whom Baudelaire repeatedly concerned himself. One year before he wrote 'Le Vin des chiffonniers' he published a prose presentation of the figure: 'Here we have a man who has to gather the day's refuse in the capital city. Everything that the big city threw away, everything it lost, everything it despised, everything it crushed underfoot, he catalogues and collects. He collates the annals of intemperance, the *capharnaüm* (stockpile) of waste. He sorts things out and makes a wise choice; he collects, like a miser guarding a treasure, the refuse which will assume the shape of useful or gratifying objects between the jaws of the goddess of Industry.'[38] This description is one

37. Gabriel Bounoure, 'Abîmes de Victor Hugo', in *Mesures*, 15 July 1936, p. 40.   38. I, 249ff.

extended metaphor for the procedure of the poet in Baudelaire's spirit. Ragpicker or poet – the refuse concerns both, and both go about their business in solitude at times when the citizens indulge in sleeping; even the gesture is the same with both. Nadar speaks of Baudelaire's 'jerky gait' (*'pas saccadé'*).[39] This is the gait of the poet who roams the city in search of rhyme-booty; it must also be the gait of the ragpicker who stops on his path every few moments to pick up the refuse he encounters. There is much to indicate that Baudelaire secretly wished to bring this relationship out. It contains a prophecy in any case. Sixty years later a brother of the poet who has deteriorated into a ragpicker appears in Apollinaire. It is Croniamantal, the *poète assassiné*, the first victim of the pogrom that is intended to end the species of the lyric poets in the entire world.

The poetry of apachedom appears in an uncertain light. Do the dregs of society supply the heroes of the big city? Or is the hero the poet who fashions his work from such material?[40] The theory of modernism admits both. But in a late poem, 'Les Plaintes d'un Icare', the ageing Baudelaire indicates that he no longer feels with the kind of people among whom he sought heroes in his youth.

> Les amants des prostituées
> Sont heureux, dispos et repus;
> Quant à moi, mes bras sont rompus
> Pour avoir étreint des nuées.[41]

> (Who gives a prostitute his love
> Is happy, satisfied and free;
> My arms are broken utterly
> For having clasped the clouds above.)

translated by Lewis Piaget Shanks

The poet, who, as the poem's title indicates, is the stand-in for the ancient hero, has had to give way to the modern hero whose deeds

39. Quoted in Firmin Maillard, *La cité des intellectuels*, Paris, 1905, p. 362.
40. For a long time Baudelaire intended to produce novels from this milieu. Among his posthumous papers there were traces of such plans in the form of titles: *Les enseignements d'un monstre*, *L'entreteneur*, *La femme malhonnête*.
41. I, 193.

are reported by the *Gazette des Tribunaux*.[42] In actuality this resignation is already inherent in the concept of the modern hero. He is predestined for doom, and no tragedian need come forward to set forth the necessary for this downfall. But once modernism has received its due, its time has run out. Then it will be put to the test. After its end it will become apparent whether it will ever be able to become antiquity.

Baudelaire always remained aware of this question. He experienced the ancient claim to immortality as his claim to being read as an ancient writer some day. 'That all *modernism* is worthy of becoming antiquity some day'[43] – to him that defined the artistic mission generally. In Baudelaire Gustave Kahn very aptly noticed a *'refus de l'occasion, tendu par la nature du prétexte lyrique'*.[44] What made him indifferent towards opportunities and occasions was the consciousness of that mission. In the epoch to which he belonged, nothing came closer to the 'task' of the ancient hero, to the 'labours' of a Hercules than the task imposed upon him as his very own; to give shape to modernity.

Among all relationships into which modernity entered, its relationship to classical antiquity stands out. For Baudelaire this could be seen in the works of Victor Hugo. 'Fate led him . . . to remodel the classical ode and classical tragedy . . . into the poems and the dramas which we know by him.'[45] Modernity designates an epoch, and it also denotes the energies which are at work in this epoch to bring it close to antiquity. Baudelaire conceded such energies to Hugo reluctantly and in only a few cases. Wagner, on the other hand, appeared to him as an unbounded, unadulterated effusion of this energy. 'If in the choice of his subjects and his dramatic method Wagner approaches classical antiquity, his passionate power of expression makes him the most important representative of modernity at the present time.'[46] This sentence contains Baudelaire's theory of modern art in a nutshell. In his view, the quality of antiquity is limited to the construction; the substance and the inspiration of a

---

42. Three-quarters of a century later the confrontation between the pimp and the man of letters was revitalized. When the writers were driven out of Germany, a Horst Wessel legend entered German literature.

43. II, 336.   44. Kahn, op. cit., p. 15.   45. II, 580.
46. II, 508.

work are the concern of modernism. 'Woe to him who studies other aspects of antiquity than pure art, logic, the general method. He who becomes excessively absorbed in antiquity, divests himself of the privileges opportunity offers him.'[47] And in the final passage of his essay on Guys he says: 'Everywhere he sought the transitory, fleeting beauty of our present life, the character of what the reader has permitted us to call *modernism*.'[48] In summary form, his doctrine reads as follows: 'A constant, unchangeable element . . . and a relative, limited element cooperates to produce beauty. . . . The latter element is supplied by the epoch, by fashion, by morality, and the passions. Without this second element . . . the first would not be assimilable.'[49] One cannot say that this is a profound analysis.

In Baudelaire's view of modernism, the theory of modern art is the weakest point. His general view brings out the modern themes; his theory of art should probably have concerned itself with classical art, but Baudelaire never attempted anything of the kind. His theory did not cope with the resignation which in his work appears as a loss of nature and naïveté. Its dependence on Poe down to its formulation is one expression of its constraint. Its polemical orientation is another; it stands out against the grey background of historicism, against the academic Alexandrinism which was in vogue with Villemain and Cousin. None of the aesthetic reflections in Baudelaire's theory of art presented modernism in its interpenetration with classical antiquity, something that was done in certain poems of the *Fleurs du mal*.

Among these the poem 'Le Cygne' is paramount. It is no accident that it is an allegory. The city which is in constant flux grows rigid. It becomes as brittle and as transparent as glass – that is, as far as its meaning is concerned – 'The form of a city, alas, changes more quickly than a mortal's heart' ('*La forme d'une ville/Change plus vite, hélas! que le coeur d'un mortel*').[50] The stature of Paris is fragile; it is surrounded by symbols of fragility – living creatures (the negress and the swan) and historical figures (Andromache, 'widow of Hector and wife of Helenus'). Their common feature is sadness about what was and lack of hope for what is to come. In the final analysis, this decrepitude constitutes the closest connection between modernism and antiquity. Wherever Paris occurs in the

47. II, 337.   48. II, 363.   49. II, 326.   50. I, 99.

Fleurs du mal, it bears the signs of this decrepitude. 'Le Crépuscule du matin' is the sobbing of an awakening person reproduced through the material of a city. 'Le Soleil' shows the city threadbare, like an old fabric in the sunlight. The old man who resignedly reaches for his tools day after day because even in his old age he has not been freed from want is the allegory of the city, and among its inhabitants old women – 'Les Petites vieilles' – are the only spiritualized ones. That these poems have travelled through the decades unchallenged, they owe to a reservation which guards them. It is the reservation against the big city, and it differentiates them from almost all later big-city poetry. A stanza by Verhaeren suffices to understand what is involved here.

> Et qu'importent les maux et les heures démentes
> Et les cuves de vice où la cité fermente
> Si quelque jour, du fond des brouillards et des voiles
> Surgit un nouveau Christ, en lumière sculpté
> Qui soulève vers lui l'humanité
> Et la baptise au feu de nouvelles étoiles.[51]

> (And of what consequence are the evils and the lunatic hours and the vats of vice in which the city ferments, if some day a new Christ arises from the fog and the veils in a sculpted light, lifts humanity toward himself and baptizes it by the fire of new stars?)

Baudelaire knows no such perspectives. His idea of the decrepitude of the big city is the basis of the permanence of the poems which he has written about Paris.

The poem 'Le Cygne', too, is dedicated to Hugo, one of the few men whose work, it seemed to Baudelaire, produced a new antiquity. To the extent that one can speak of a source of inspiration in Hugo's case, it was fundamentally different from Baudelaire's. Hugo did not know the capacity to become rigid which – if a biological term may be used – manifests itself a hundredfold in Baudelaire's writings as a kind of mimesis of death. On the other hand, it is possible to speak of Hugo's chthonian bent. Although it is not specifically mentioned, it is brought out in the following

51. Emile Verhaeren, *Les villes tentaculaires*, Paris, 1904, p. 119 ('L'âme de la ville').

remarks by Charles Péguy which reveal where the difference between Hugo's and Baudelaire's conceptions of classical antiquity lies. 'One thing one may be sure of: when Hugo saw a beggar by the road, he saw him the way he is, really saw him the way he really is . . . saw him, the ancient beggar, the ancient supplicant, on the ancient road. When he saw the marble inlay of one of our fireplaces or the cemented bricks on one of our modern fireplaces, he saw them as what they are – namely, the stones from the hearth, the stones from the ancient hearth. When he saw the door of a house and the threshold, which is usually a squared stone, he recognized in this squared stone the antique line, the line of the sacred threshold which it is.'[52] There is no better commentary on the following passage of *Les Misérables*: 'The taverns of the Faubourg Saint-Antoine resembled the taverns of the Aventine which are built over the sibyl's cave and are connected with the sacred inspirations; the tables of these taverns were almost tripods, and Ennius speaks of the sibylline wine that was drunk there.'[53] The same way of viewing things gave birth to the work in which the first image of a 'Parisian antiquity' appears, Hugo's poetic cycle *A l'arc de triomphe*. The glorification of this architectural monument proceeds from the vision of a Paris Campagna, an *'immense campagne'* in which only three monuments of the vanished city have survived: the Sainte-Chapelle, the Vendôme column, and the Arc de Triomphe. The great significance which this cycle has in the work of Victor Hugo corresponds to the position that it occupies in the genesis of a picture of Paris in the nineteenth century which is modelled upon classical antiquity. Baudelaire undoubtedly knew this cycle which was written in 1837.

Seven years earlier the historian Friedrich von Raumer wrote in his letters from Paris and France in the year 1830: 'Yesterday I surveyed the enormous city from the Notre Dame tower. Who built the first house, when will the last one collapse and the ground of Paris look like the ground of Thebes and Babylon?'[54] Hugo has described this soil as it will be one day when 'this bank where the

52. Charles Péguy, *Oeuvres de prose*, Paris, 1916, pp. 388ff.

53. Victor Hugo, *Les Misérables*, Paris, 1881, pp. 55ff.

54. Friedrich von Raumer, *Briefe aus Paris und Frankreich im Jahre 1830*, Leipzig, 1831, vol. 2, p. 127.

water surges against resounding bridge-arches will have been restored to the murmuring, bending rushes':[55]

> Mais non, tout sera mort. Plus rien dans cette plaine
> Qu'un peuple évanoui dont elle est encore pleine.[56]

> (But no, everything will be dead. Nothing more in this plain than a vanished people with which it is still pregnant.)

A hundred years after Raumer, Léon Daudet took a look at Paris from the Sacré-Coeur, another elevated place in the city. In his eyes the history of 'modernism' up to that time was mirrored in a frightening contraction: 'From above one looks down on this agglomeration of palaces, monuments, houses, and barracks, and one gets the feeling that they are predestined for a catastrophe or several, meteorological or social. . . . I have spent hours on Four-vières with a view of Lyons, on Notre-Dame de la Garde with a view of Marseille, on the Sacré Coeur with a view of Paris. . . . What becomes most clearly recognizable from these heights is a threat. The agglomerations of human beings are threatening. . . . A man needs work, that is correct, but he has other needs, too. . . . Among his other needs there is suicide, something that is inherent in him and in the society which forms him, and it is stronger than his drive of self-preservation. Thus, when one stands on Sacré-Coeur, Fourvières, and Notre-Dame de la Garde and looks down, one is surprised that Paris, Lyons, and Marseille are still there.'[57] This is the face that the *passion moderne* which Baudelaire recognized in suicide has received in this century.

The city of Paris entered this century in the form which Hauss-mann gave it. He had revolutionized the physiognomy of the city with the most modest means imaginable: spades, pickaxes, crow-bars, and the like. What measure of destruction had been caused by even these limited instruments! And along with the growth of the big cities there developed the means of razing them to the ground. What visions of the future are evoked by this! Haussmann's activity was at its height and entire sections were being torn down when Maxime Du Camp found himself on the Pont Neuf one afternoon in 1862. He was waiting for his eyeglasses near an optician's shop.

55. Hugo, *Poésie III*, Paris, 1880.   56. ibid.
57. Léon Daudet, *Paris vécu*, Paris, 1929, vol. 1, pp. 220ff.

'The author, who was at the threshold of old age, experienced one of those moments in which a man who thinks about his past life finds his own melancholy reflected in everything. The slight deterioration of his eyesight which had been demonstrated on his visit to the optician reminded him of the law of the inevitable infirmity of all human things. . . . It suddenly occurred to the man who had travelled widely in the Orient, who was acquainted with the deserts whose sand is the dust of the dead, that this city, too, whose bustle was all around him, would have to die some day, the way so many capitals had died. It occurred to him how extraordinarily interesting an accurate description of Athens at the time of Pericles, Carthage at the time of Barca, Alexandria at the time of the Ptolemies, and Rome at the time of the Caesars would be to us today. . . . In a flash of inspiration, of the kind that occasionally brings one an extraordinary subject, he resolved to write the kind of book about Paris that the historians of antiquity failed to write about their cities. . . . In his mind's eye he could see the work of his mature old age.'[58] In Hugo's *A l'Arc de Triomphe* and in Du Camp's great presentation of his city from the administrative point of view, the same inspiration is discernable that became decisive for Baudelaire's idea of modernism.

Haussmann set to work in 1859. His work had long been regarded as necessary and the way for it had been prepared by legislation. 'After 1848,' wrote Du Camp in the above-mentioned work, 'Paris was about to become uninhabitable. The constant expansion of the railway network . . . accelerated traffic and an increase in the city's population. The people choked in the narrow, dirty, convoluted old streets where they remained packed in because there was no other way.'[59] At the beginning of the fifties the population of Paris began to accommodate itself to the idea that a great face-cleaning of the city was inevitable. It may be assumed that in its incubation period this clean-up could have at least as great an effect upon a good imagination as the work of urban

58. Paul Bourget, 'Discours académique du 13 juin 1895. Succession à Maxime Du Camp', in *L'anthologie de l'Académie française*, Paris, 1921, vol. 2, pp. 191ff.

59. Maxime Du Camp, *Paris, ses organes, ses fonctions et sa vie dans la seconde moitié du XIXe siècle*, vol. 6, Paris, 1886, p. 253.

renewal itself. 'Poets are more inspired by the image than by the actual presence of objects' ('*Les poètes sont plus inspirés par les images que par la présence même des objets*'), said Joubert.[60] The same is true of artists. Anything about which one knows that one soon will not have it around becomes an image. Presumably this is what happened to the streets of Paris at that time. In any case, the work whose subterranean connection with the great remodelling of Paris is least to be doubted, was finished a few years before this remodelling was undertaken. It was Meryon's engraved views of Paris. No one was more impressed with them than Baudelaire. To him the archaeological view of the catastrophe, the basis of Hugo's dreams, was not the really moving one. For him antiquity was to spring suddenly like an Athena from the head of an unhurt Zeus, from an intact modernism. Meryon brought out the ancient face of the city without abandoning one cobblestone. It was this view of the matter that Baudelaire had unceasingly pursued in the idea of modernism. He was a passionate admirer of Meryon.

The two men had an elective affinity to each other. They were born in the same year, and their deaths were only months apart. Both died lonely and deeply disturbed – Meryon as a demented person at Charenton, Baudelaire speechless in a private clinic. Both were late in achieving fame.[61] Baudelaire was almost the only person who championed Meryon in his lifetime. Few of his prose works are a match for his short piece on Meryon. Dealing with Meryon, it is a homage to modernism, but it is also a homage to the antique aspects of Meryon. For in Meryon, too, there is an interpenetration of classical antiquity and modernism, and in him the form of this superimposition, the allegory, appears unmistakably. The captions under his etchings are of importance. If the texts are touched by madness, their obscurity only underlines the 'meaning'. As an interpretation, Meryon's verses under his view of the Pont Neuf are, despite their sophistry, closely related to the 'Squelette laboureur':

60. Joseph Joubert, *Pensées précédées de sa correspondance*, Paris, 1883, vol. 2, p. 267.

61. In the twentieth century Meryon found a biographer in Gustave Geffroy. It is no accident that the masterpiece of this author is a biography of Blanqui.

Ci-gît du vieux Pont Neuf
L'exact ressemblance
Tout radoubé de neuf
Par récente ordonnance.
O savants médecins,
Habiles chirurgiens,
De nous pourquoi ne faire
Comme du pont de pierre.[62]

(Here lies the exact likeness of the old Pont
Neuf, all recaulked like new in accordance with a
recent ordinance. O learned physicians and skil-
ful surgeons, why not do with us as was done
with this stone bridge.)

In seeing the uniqueness of these pictures in the fact 'that, although
they are made directly from life, they give an impression of expired
life, something that is dead or is going to die',[63] Geffroy under-
stands the essence of Meryon's work as well as its relationship to
Baudelaire, and he is particularly aware of the faithfulness with
which the city of Paris is reproduced, a city that was soon to be
pockmarked with rubble fields. Baudelaire's Meryon essay contains
a subtle reference to the significance of this Paris antiquity. 'Seldom
have we seen the natural solemnity of a great city depicted with
more poetic power: the majesty of the piles of stone; those spires
pointing their fingers to the sky; the obelisks of industry vomiting

62. Quoted in Gustave Geffroy, *Charles Meryon*, Paris, 1926, p. 2. Meryon
began as a naval officer. His last etching presents the navy ministry on the
Place de la Concorde. A train of horses, carriages, and dolphins is shown in
the clouds rushing toward the ministry. There are ships and sea serpents, too,
and some creatures of human form may be seen in the crowd. Geffroy easily
finds the 'meaning' without dwelling on the form or the allegory: 'His dreams
rushed up to this house which was as solid as a fortress. That is where the
record of his career had been entered in his youth, when he was still embarked
on great travels. And now he bids farewell to this city and this house which
have caused him so much suffering' (Gustave Geffroy, op. cit., p. 161).

63. ibid. The will to preserve the 'traces' is most decisively involved in this
art. Meryon's title for his series of etchings shows a loose rock bearing the
imprinted traces of old plant forms.

a legion of smoke against the heavens;[64] the enormous scaffolds of the monuments under repair, pressing the spider-web-like and paradoxical beauty of their structure against the monuments' solid bodies; the steamy sky, pregnant with rage and heavy with rancour; and the wide vistas whose poetry resides in the dramas with which one endows them in one's imagination – none of the complex elements that compose the painful and glorious décor of civilization has been forgotten.'[65] Among the plans whose failure one can mourn like a loss is that of the publisher Delâtre who wanted to issue Meryon's series with texts by Baudelaire. That these texts were never written was the fault of the artist; he was incapable of conceiving of Baudelaire's task as anything else than an inventory of the houses and streets depicted by him. If Baudelaire had undertaken that assignment, Proust's remark about 'the role of the ancient cities in the work of Baudelaire and the scarlet colour which they occasionally give it'[66] would make more sense than it does today. Among these cities Rome was paramount for him. In a letter to Leconte de Lisle he confesses his 'natural predilection' for that city. It probably stems from the etchings (*veduta*) of Piranesi on which the non-restored ruins and the new city still appear as one.

The sonnet which constitutes the thirty-ninth poem of the *Fleurs du mal* begins as follows:

> Je te donne ces vers afin que si mon nom
> Aborde heureusement aux époques lointaines,
> Et fait rêver un soir les cervelles humaines,
> Vaisseau favorisé par un grand aquilon,
>
> Ta mémoire, pareille aux fables incertaines,
> Fatigue le lecteur ainsi qu'un tympanon.[67]
>
> (I give this verse to you in case my name,
> A vessel favoured by a strong north wind,
> Lands in distant epochs with some fame
> And brings a dream at evening to man's mind;

64. cf. Pierre Hamp's reproachful remark: 'The artist . . . admires the column of the Babylonian temple and despises a factory chimney' (Pierre Hamp, 'La littérature, image de la société', in *Encyclopédie française*, vol. 16: *Arts et littératures dans la société contemporaine*, I, Paris, 1935, fasc. 16.64–1).

65. II, 293.   66. Proust, op. cit., p. 656.   67. I, 53.

> Thus you, as in some vague old tale, may tease
> The reader like a dulcimer's thin chimes.)

translated by C. F. MacIntyre

Baudelaire wanted to be read like a classical poet. This claim fell due with astonishing speed, for the distant future, the *époques lointaines* mentioned in the sonnet, has arrived – as many decades after his death as Baudelaire may have imagined centuries. To be sure, Paris is still standing and the great tendencies of social development are still the same. But the more constant they have remained, the more obsolete has everything that was in the sign of the 'truly new' been rendered by the experience of them. Modernism has changed most of all, and the antiquity that it was supposed to contain really presents the picture of the obsolete. 'Herculaneum is found again under the ashes; but a few years bury the mores of a society more effectively than all the dust of the volcanoes.'[68]

Baudelaire's antiquity is Roman antiquity. In only one place does Greek antiquity extend into his world. Greece supplies him with the image of the heroine which seemed to him worthy and capable of being carried over into modern times. In one of the greatest and most famous poems of the *Fleurs du mal* the women bear Greek names, Delphine and Hippolyte. The poem is devoted to lesbian love. The lesbian is the heroine of modernism. In her an erotic ideal of Baudelaire – the woman who bespeaks hardness and mannishness – has combined with a historical ideal, that of greatness in the ancient world. This makes the position of the lesbian in the *Fleurs du mal* unmistakable. It explains why Baudelaire for a long time had the title *Les Lesbiennes* in mind. Incidentally, Baudelaire by no means discovered the lesbian for art. In his *Fille aux yeux d'or* Balzac already knew her, and so did Gautier in *Mademoiselle de Maupin* and Delatouche in *Fragoletta*. Baudelaire also encountered her in the work of Delacroix; in a critique of his pictures he speaks, somewhat circuitously, of 'the modern woman in her heroic manifestation, in the sense of infernal or divine'.[69]

The motif may be found in Saint-Simonism which in its cultic

68. Barbey d'Aurevilly, 'Du dandysme et de G. Brummel', in *Memoranda*, Paris, 1887, p. 30.
69. II, 162.

velleities often utilized the idea of the androgyne. One of these is the temple which was to be a showpiece of Duveyrier's 'New City'. A disciple of the school wrote about it as follows: 'The temple must represent an androgyne, a man and a woman. . . . The same division must be planned for the entire city, even the entire kingdom and the whole earth. There will be a hemisphere of man and a hemisphere of woman.'[70] As far as its anthropological content is concerned, the Saint-Simonian utopia is more comprehensible in the ideas of Claire Démar than in this architecture which was never built. Over the grandiloquent fantasies of Enfantin, Claire Démar has been forgotten. Yet the manifesto that she left behind is closer to the essence of the Saint-Simonian theory – the hypostatization of industry as the force that moves the world – than is Enfantin's mother-myth. Her text, too, is concerned with the mother, but in a sense substantially different from those who set out from France to seek her in the Orient. In the widely ramified literature of the time which deals with the future of women, Démar's manifesto is unique in its power and passion. It appeared under the title *Ma loi d'avenir*. In the concluding section she writes: 'No more motherhood! No law of the blood. I say: no more motherhood. Once a woman has been freed from men who pay her the price of her body . . . she will owe her existence . . . only to her own creativity. To this end she must devote herself to a work and fulfil a function. . . . So you will have to decide to take a newborn child from the breast of its natural mother and place it in the hands of a social mother, a nurse employed by the state. In this way the child will be raised better. . . . Only then and not earlier will men, women, and children be freed from the law of blood, the law of mankind's self-exploitation.'[71]

Here the image of the heroic woman which Baudelaire absorbed may be seen in its original version. Its lesbian variant was not the work of the writers but that of the Saint-Simonian circle. Whatever documentation is involved here surely was not in the best of hands with the chroniclers of this school. However, we do have the following peculiar confession by a woman who was one of the

70. Henry-René de Allemagne, *Les Saint-Simoniens 1827–1837*, Paris, 1930, p. 310.
71. Claire Démar, *Ma loi d'avenir. Ouvrage posthume publié par Suzanne*, Paris, 1834, pp. 58ff.

adherents of Saint-Simon's doctrine: 'I began to love my fellow woman as much as I loved my fellow man. . . . I conceded the physical strength of men as well as the kind of intelligence that is peculiar to them, but placed alongside him as his equal the physical beauty of women and the intellectual gifts peculiar to them.'[72] A critical reflection by Baudelaire which one would not have expected sounds like an echo of this confession. It concerns itself with Flaubert's first heroine. 'In her optimal vigour and her most ambitious goals as well as in her deepest dreams, Madame Bovary . . . has remained a man. Like Pallas Athene, who sprang from the head of Zeus, this strange androgyne has been given all the seductive power of a masculine spirit in an enchanting woman's body.'[73] And about the author himself he writes: 'All *intellectual* women will be grateful to him for having raised the "little woman" to such a high level . . . and to have her participate in the dual nature that makes up a perfect human being: to be as capable of calculation as of dreaming.'[74] With the kind of *coup de main* that was appropriate to him, Baudelaire raises Flaubert's petty-bourgeois wife to the status of a heroine.

In Baudelaire's work there are a number of important and even evident facts that have remained unnoticed. Among them is the antithetical orientation of the two lesbian poems that succeed each other in the *Épaves*. 'Lesbos' is a hymn to lesbian love; 'Delphine et Hippolyte', on the other hand, is a condemnation of this passion, whatever the nature of the compassion that animates it.

> Que nous veulent les lois du juste et de l'injuste?
> Vierges au coeur sublime, honneur de l'Archipel,
> Votre religion comme une autre est auguste,
> Et l'amour se rira de l'Enfer et du Ciel![75]

> (What boot the laws of just and of unjust?
> Great-hearted virgins, honour of the isles,
> Lo, your religion also is august,
> And love at hell and heaven together smiles!)

translated by Richard Herne Shepherd

72. Quoted in Maillard, *La légende de la femme émancipée*, Paris, n.d., p. 65.
73. II, 445.   74. II, 448.   75. I, 157.

These lines are taken from the first poem. In the second poem Baudelaire says:

> – Descendez, descendez, lamentables victimes,
> Descendez le chemin de l'enfer éternel![76]

> (Hence, lamentable victims, get you hence!
> Hells yawn beneath, your road is straight and steep.)

translated by Aldous Huxley

This striking dichotomy may be explained as follows. Just as Baudelaire did not view the lesbian as either a social or a physical problem, he had no attitude towards her in real life, as it were. He had room for her within the framework of modernism, but he did not recognize her in reality. That is why he wrote nonchalantly: 'We have known the female philanthropist who wrote . . ., the republican poetess, the poetess of the future, be she a Fourierist or a Saint-Simonist.[77] But we have never been able to accustom our eyes . . . to all this solemn and repulsive behaviour . . . these sacrilegious imitations of the masculine spirit.'[78] It would be erroneous to assume that it ever occurred to Baudelaire to champion lesbians publicly in his writings. This is proved by the proposals he made to his attorney for the latter's plea in the *Fleurs du mal* trial. To him, social ostracism was inseparable from the heroic nature of this passion. *'Descendez, descendez, lamentables victimes'* were the last words that Baudelaire addressed to lesbians. He abandoned them to their doom, and they could not be saved, because the confusion in Baudelaire's conception of them is inextricable.

The nineteenth century began to use women without reservation in the production process outside the home. It did so primarily in a primitive fashion by putting them into factories. Consequently, in the course of time masculine traits were bound to manifest themselves in these women. These were caused particularly by disfiguring factory work. Higher forms of production as well as the political struggle as such were able to promote masculine features of a more refined nature. The movement of the Vésuviennes can

76. I, 161.
77. This may be an allusion to Claire Démar's *Ma loi d'avenir.*
78. II, 534.

perhaps be understood in such a way. It supplied the February Revolution with a corps composed of women. 'We call ourselves Vésuviennes,' it says in the statutes, 'to indicate that a revolutionary volcano is at work in every woman who belongs to our group.'[79] Such a change of the feminine habitus brought out tendencies which were capable of engaging Baudelaire's imagination. It would not be surprising if his profound antipathy to pregnancy had been involved.[80] The masculinization of woman was in keeping with it, so Baudelaire approved of the process. At the same time, however, he sought to free it from economic bondage. Thus he reached the point where he gave a purely sexual accent to this development. What he could not forgive George Sand was perhaps that she had desecrated the features of a lesbian by her affair with Musset.

The deterioration of the 'realistic' element which is evident in Baudelaire's attitude towards lesbians is characteristic of him in other things as well. It struck attentive observers as strange. In 1895 Jules Lemaître wrote: 'One confronts a work full of artifice and intentional contradictions. . . . Even as he gives the crassest descriptions of the bleakest details of reality, he indulges in a spiritualism which greatly distracts us from the immediate impression that things make upon us. . . . Baudelaire regards a woman as a slave or animal, but he renders her the same homage as he does to the Holy Virgin. . . . He curses "progress", he loathes the industry of the century, and yet he enjoys the special flavour which this industry has given today's life. . . . I believe the specifically Baudelairean is the constant combination of two opposite modes of reaction . . . one could call it a past and a present mode. A masterpiece of the will . . . the latest innovation in the sphere of emotional life.'[81] To present this attitude as a great achievement of the will was in Baudelaire's spirit. But the other side of the coin is a lack of conviction, insight, and steadiness. In all his stirrings Baudelaire was subject to an abrupt, shock-like change, so his vision of another

79. *Paris sous la République de 1848. Exposition de la Bibliothèque et des travaux historiques de la ville de Paris*, Paris, 1909, p. 28.

80. A fragment of 1844 (I, 213) seems pertinent here. Baudelaire's well-known drawing of his mistress shows a gait bearing a striking resemblance to the gait of a pregnant woman. This does not disprove his antipathy.

81. Jules Lemaître, *Les contemporains*, Paris, 1895, pp. 29ff.

way of living in the extremes was all the more alluring. This way
takes shape in the incantations which emanate from many of his
perfect verses; in some of them it names itself.

> Vois sur ces canaux
> Dormir ces vaisseaux
> Dont l'humeur est vagabonde;
> C'est pour assouvir
> Ton moindre désir
> Qu'ils viennent du bout du monde.[82]

> (See, sheltered from the swells
> There in the still canals
> Those drowsy ships that dream of sailing forth;
> It is to satisfy
> Your least desire, they ply
> Hither through all the waters of the earth.)

translated by Richard Wilbur

This famous stanza has a rocking rhythm; its movement seizes the
ships which lie fast in the canals. To be rocked between the extremes, as is the privilege of ships – that is what Baudelaire longed
for. The ships emerge where the profound, secret, and paradoxical
image of his dreams is involved: being supported and sheltered
by greatness. 'These beautiful big ships that lie on the still water
imperceptibly rocking, these strong ships that look so idle and so
nostalgic – are they not asking us in a mute language: when are we
setting out for happiness?'[83] In the ships, nonchalance is combined
with readiness for the utmost exertion of energy. This gives them a
secret significance. There is a special constellation in which greatness and indolence meet in human beings, too. This constellation
governed Baudelaire's life. He deciphered it and called it 'modernism'. When he loses himself to the spectacle of the ships lying at
anchor, he does so in order to derive an allegory from them. The
hero is as strong, as ingenious, as harmonious, and as well-built
as those boats. But the high seas beckon to him in vain, for his life
is under an ill star. Modernism turns out to be his doom. The hero

82. I, 67.   83. II, 630.

was not provided for in it; it has no use for this type. It makes him fast in the secure harbour forever and abandons him to everlasting idleness. In this, his last embodiment, the hero appears as a dandy. If one encounters one of these figures who, thanks to their strength and composure, are perfect in their every gesture, one says to oneself, 'Here is perhaps a rich man; but more certainly a Hercules with no work.'[84] He seems to be supported by his greatness. Hence it is understandable that at certain times Baudelaire thought his strolling was endowed with the same dignity as the exertion of his poetic power.

To Baudelaire the dandy appeared to be a descendant of great ancestors. For him dandyism was 'the last shimmer of the heroic in times of decadence'.[85] It pleased him to discover in Chateaubriand a reference to Indian dandies – evidence of a past flowering of those tribes. In truth it must be recognized that the features which are combined in the dandy bear a very definite historical stamp. The dandy is a creation of the English who were leaders in world trade. The trade network that spans the globe was in the hands of the London stock-exchange people; its meshes felt the most varied, most frequent, most unforeseeable tremors. A merchant had to react to these, but he could not publicly display his reactions. The dandies took charge of the conflicts thus created. They developed the ingenious training that was necessary to overcome these conflicts. They combined an extremely quick reaction with a relaxed, even slack demeanour and facial expression. The tic, which for a time was regarded as fashionable, is, as it were, the clumsy, low-level presentation of the problem. The following statement is very revealing: 'The face of an elegant man must always have something convulsive and distorted. Such a grimace can, if one wishes, be ascribed to a natural satanism.'[86] This is how the figure of the London dandy appeared in the mind of a Paris boulevardier, and this was its physiognomic reflection in Baudelaire. His love for dandyism was not successful. He did not have the gift of pleasing, which is such an important element in the dandy's art of not pleasing. Turning the things about him that by nature had to strike one as strange into

84. II, 352.   85. II, 351.
86 Taxile Delord et al., *Les Petits-Paris. Par les auteurs des 'Memoires de Bilboquet'*, Paris, 1854; vol. 10, *Paris, viveur*, pp. 25ff.

a mannerism, he became profoundly lonely, particularly since his inaccessibility increased as he became more isolated.

Unlike Gautier, Baudelaire found nothing to like about his time, and unlike Leconte de Lisle he was unable to deceive himself about it. He did not have the humanitarian idealism of a Lamartine or a Hugo, and it was not given to him, as it was to Verlaine, to take refuge in religious devotion. Because he did not have any convictions, he assumed ever new forms himself. *Flâneur*, apache, dandy and ragpicker were so many roles to him. For the modern hero is no hero; he acts heroes. Heroic modernism turns out to be a tragedy in which the hero's part is available. Baudelaire indicated this, half-hidden in a *remarque*, in his poem 'Les Sept vieillards'.

> Un matin, cependant que dans la triste rue
> Les maisons, dont la brume allongeait la hauteur,
> Simulaient les deux quais d'une rivière accrue,
> Et que, décor semblable à l'âme de l'acteur,
>
> Un brouillard sale et jaune inondait tout l'espace,
> Je suivais, roidissant mes nerfs comme un héros
> Et discutant avec mon âme déjà lasse,
> Le faubourg secoué pas les lourds tombereaux.[87]

> (One early morning, in the street's sad mud,
> Whose houses, by the fog increased in height,
> Seemed wharves along a riverside in flood:
> When with a scene to match the actor's plight,
>
> Foul yellow mist had filled the whole of space:
> Steeling my nerves to play a hero's part,
> I coaxed my weary soul with me to pace
> The backstreets shaken by each lumbering cart.)

translated by Roy Campbell

The decor, the actor, and the hero meet in these stanzas in an unmistakable way. Baudelaire's contemporaries did not need the reference. When Courbet was painting Baudelaire, he complained that his subject looked different every day. And Champfleury said that Baudelaire had the ability to change his facial expression like a

87. I, 101.

fugitive from a chain gang.[88] In his malicious obituary, which evidences a fair amount of acuity, Vallès called Baudelaire a *cabotin*[99] [ham actor].

Behind the masks which he used up, the poet in Baudelaire preserved his incognito. He was as circumspect in his work as he was capable of seeming provocative in his personal associations. The incognito was the law of his poetry. His prosody is comparable to the map of a big city in which it is possible to move about inconspicuously, shielded by blocks of houses, gateways, courtyards. On this map the places for the words are clearly indicated, as the places are indicated for conspirators before the outbreak of a revolt. Baudelaire conspires with language itself. He calculates its effects step by step. That he always avoided revealing himself to the reader has been noticed particularly by the most competent observers. Gide noticed a very calculated disharmony between the image and the object.[90] Rivière has emphasized how Baudelaire proceeds from the remote word, how he reaches it to tread softly as he cautiously brings it closer to the object.[91] Lemaître speaks of forms which are constituted so as to check an eruption of passion,[92] and Laforgue emphasizes Baudelaire's similes which, as it were, give the lie to the lyrical person and get into the text as disturbing intruders. Laforgue quotes 'The night thickened like a partition' ('*La nuit s'épaississait ainsi qu'une cloison*'),[93] and adds: 'A wealth of other examples could be found'.[94]

88. cf. Champfleury [Jules Husson], *Souvenirs et portraits de jeunesse*, Paris, 1872, p. 135.

89. Reprinted from *La situation* in André Billy, *Les écrivains de combat*, Paris, 1931, p. 189.

90. cf. Gide, op. cit., p. 512.

91. cf. Jacques Rivière, *Études* [Paris, 1948, p. 15].

92. cf. Lemaître, op. cit., p. 29.

93. Jules Laforgue, *Mélanges posthumes*, Paris, 1903, p. 113.

94. From this wealth the following may be cited:

> Nous volons au passage un plaisir clandestin
> Que nous pressons bien fort comme une vieille orange (I, 17).
>
> (We hastily steal a clandestine pleasure
> Which we squeeze very hard like an old orange.)
>
> Ta gorge triomphante est une belle armoire (I, 65).
>
> (Your triumphant bosom is a fine wardrobe.)

The division of words into those that seemed suitable for elevated speech, and those that were to be excluded from it, influenced poetic production generally and from the beginning applied to tragedy no less than to lyric poetry. In the first decades of the nineteenth century this convention was in undisputed force. When Lebrun's *Cid* was performed, the word *chambre* evoked mutterings of disapproval. *Othello*, in Alfred de Vigny's translation, failed because of the word *mouchoir* whose mention seemed unbearable in a tragedy. Victor Hugo had begun smoothing out the difference in literature between the words of colloquial language and those of elevated speech. Sainte-Beuve had proceeded in a similar fashion. In his life of Joseph Delorme he explained: 'I have tried to be original in my own way, in a modest, homely way. I called the things of intimate life by their names; but in doing so a hut was closer to me than a boudoir.'[95] Baudelaire transcended both Victor Hugo's linguistic Jacobinism and Sainte-Beuve's bucolic liberties. His images are original by virtue of the inferiority of the objects of comparison. He is on the lookout for banal incidents in order to approximate them to poetic events. He speaks of the 'vague terrors of those frightful nights which compress the heart the way a piece of paper is crumpled' (*'vagues terreurs de ces affreuses nuits/Qui compriment le coeur comme un papier qu'on froisse'*).[96] This linguistic gesture, characteristic of the artist in Baudelaire, becomes truly significant only in the

> Comme un sanglot coupé par un sang écumeux
> Le chant du coq au loin déchirait l'air brumeux (I, 118).

> (The distant cock-crow rent the hazy air like a sob
> stifled by frothy blood.)

> La tête, avec l'amas de sa crinière sombre
> Et de ses bijoux précieux,
> Sur la table de nuit, comme une renoncule,
> Repose (I, 126).

> (The head with the mass of its dark mane and its
> precious jewels rests on the night-table like a ranunculus.)

95. Charles-Augustin Saint-Beuve, *Vie, poésies et pensées de Joseph Delorme*, Paris, 1863, vol. 1, p. 170.
96. I, 57.

allegorist. It gives his allegory the confusing quality that distinguishes it from the ordinary kind. Lemercier had been the last to populate the Parnassus of the Empire with such allegories, and the nadir of neoclassical literature had thus been reached. Baudelaire was unconcerned about that. He took up a profusion of allegories and altered their character fundamentally by virtue of the linguistic environment in which he placed them. The *Fleurs du mal* is the first book that used in poetry not only words of ordinary provenance but words of urban origin as well. Yet Baudelaire by no means avoided locutions which, free from poetic patina, strike one with the brilliance of their coinage. He uses *quinquet*, *wagon*, or *omnibus*, and does not shrink from *bilan*, *réverbère*, or *voirie*. This is the nature of the lyric vocabulary in which an allegory appears suddenly and without prior preparation. If Baudelaire's linguistic spirit can be apprehended anywhere, it may be captured in this brusque coincidence. Claudel gave it its definitive formulation when he said that Baudelaire combined the style of Racine with the style of a journalist of the Second Empire.[97] Not a word of his vocabulary is predestined for allegory. A word is given this assignment in a particular case, depending on what is involved, what subject's turn it is to be reconnoitred, besieged, and occupied. For the *coup de main* which Baudelaire calls writing poetry, he takes allegories into his confidence. They are the only ones that have been let in on the secret. Where *la Mort* or *le Souvenir*, *le Repentir* or *le Mal* appear, centres of poetic strategy are located. The flash-like appearance of these figures, recognizable by their majuscule, in a text which does not disdain the most banal word betrays Baudelaire's hand. His technique is the technique of the *putsch*.

A few years after Baudelaire's end Blanqui crowned his career as a conspirator with a memorable feat. It was after the murder of Victor Noir. Blanqui wished to take an inventory of his troops. He knew only his lieutenants personally, and it is not certain how many of his other men knew him. He communicated with Granger, his adjutant, who made arrangements for a review of the Blanquists. Geffroy has described it as follows: 'Blanqui left his house armed, said good-bye to his sisters, and took up his post in the Champs-Elysées. According to his agreement with Granger, the troops

97. Quoted in Rivière, op. cit., p. 15.

whose mysterious general Blanqui was, were to pass in review. He knew the chiefs, and now he was supposed to see, following each of them, their people march past him in regular formation. It happened as decided upon. Blanqui held his review without anyone having any inkling of the strange spectacle. The old man stood leaning against a tree among the crowd of people who were watching just as he was, and paid close attention to his friends who came marching up in columns, approaching silently amidst murmuring which kept being interrupted by shouts.'[98] Baudelaire's poetry has preserved in words the strength that made such a thing possible.

On some occasions Baudelaire tried to recognize the image of the modern hero in the conspirator as well. 'No more tragedies!' he wrote in the *Salut public* during the February days. 'No more history of ancient Rome! Are we today not greater than Brutus?'[99] Greater than Brutus was, to be sure, less great. For when Napoleon III came to power, Baudelaire did not recognize the Caesar in him. In this Blanqui was superior to him. But that which they had in common goes deeper than the differences between them: the obstinacy and the impatience, the power of their indignation and their hatred, as well as the impotence which was the lot of both of them. In a famous line Baudelaire lightheartedly bids a world farewell 'in which action is not the sister of dreams'.[100] His dream was not as forsaken as it seemed to him. Blanqui's action was the sister of Baudelaire's dream. The two are intertwined. They are the intertwined hands on a stone under which Napoleon III buried the hopes of the June fighters.

98. Geffroy, *L'enfermé*, Paris, 1897, pp. 276ff.
99. Quoted in Eugène Crépet, *Charles Baudelaire*, Paris, 1906, p. 81.
100. I, 136.

Addendum to
'The Paris of the Second Empire
in Baudelaire'*

      Sundering truth from falsehood is the goal of the material-
ist method, not its point of departure. In other words, its point of
departure is the object riddled with error, with δοξα [conjecture].
The distinctions with which the materialist method, discriminative
from the outset, starts are distinctions within this highly mixed
object, and it cannot present this object as mixed or uncritical
enough. If it claimed to approach the object the way it is 'in truth',
it would only greatly reduce its chances. These chances, however,
are considerably augmented if the materialist method increasingly
abandons such a claim, thus preparing for the insight that 'the
matter in itself' is not 'in truth'.

    It is, to be sure, tempting to pursue the 'matter in itself'. In the
case of Baudelaire, it offers itself in profusion. The sources flow to
one's heart's content, and there they converge to form the stream
of tradition; this stream flows along as far as the eye can reach
between well-laid-out slopes. Historical materialism is not diverted
by this spectacle. It does not seek the reflection of the clouds in this

* The material which follows is a translation of Benjamin's uncompleted
methodological introduction, intended either for the Baudelaire book as a
whole or for the foregoing text, its central section. The text translated here is
that of the longer, handwritten version in the Potsdam Archive (see the
bibliographical note, page 7 above). The shorter, typescript version in
the Frankfurt Archive was published in *Kursbuch*, no. 20, Frankfurt, 1970.

stream, but it also does not turn away from the stream to drink 'from the source' and pursue the 'matter itself' behind men's backs. Whose mills does this stream activate? Who is utilizing its power? Who dammed it? These are the questions which historical materialism asks, and it changes the picture of the landscape by naming the forces which have been operative in it.

This seems like a complicated process, and it is. Is there not a more direct, a more decisive one? Why not simply confront the poet Baudelaire with present-day society and answer the question as to what he has to say to this society's progressive cadres by referring to his works – without, to be sure, ignoring the question whether he has anything to say to them at all? What speaks against this is precisely that when we read Baudelaire we are given a course of historical lessons by bourgeois society. These lessons can never be ignored. A critical reading of Baudelaire and a critical revision of this course of lessons are one and the same thing. For it is an illusion of vulgar Marxism that the social function of a material or intellectual product can be determined without reference to the circumstances and the bearers of its tradition. 'As the aggregate of objects which are viewed independently (if not of the production process in which they originated, then of the production process in which they survive), the concept of culture . . . has something fetishistic about it.'[1] The tradition of Baudelaire's works is a very short one, but it already bears historical scars which must be of interest to critical observers.

TASTE

Taste develops with the definite preponderance of commodity production over any other kind of production. As a consequence of the manufacture of products as commodities for the market, people become less and less aware of the conditions of their

1. The incalculable consequences of the more resolute procedure are rather forbidding in other respects as well. There is little point in trying to include the position of a Baudelaire in the fabric of the most advanced position in mankind's struggle of liberation. From the outset it seems more promising to investigate his machinations where he undoubtedly is at home – in the enemy camp. Very rarely are they a blessing for the opposite side. Baudelaire was a secret agent – an agent of the secret discontent of his class with its own rule.

production – not only of the social conditions in the form of exploitation, but of the technical conditions as well. The consumer, who is more or less expert when he gives an order to an artisan – in individual cases he is advised by the master craftsman himself – is not usually knowledgeable when he appears as a buyer. Added to this is the fact that mass production, which aims at turning out inexpensive commodities, must be bent upon disguising bad quality. In most cases it is actually in its interest that the buyer have little expertise. The more industry progresses, the more perfect are the imitations which it throws on the market. The commodity is bathed in a profane glow; this glow has nothing in common with the glow that produces its 'theological capers', yet it is of some importance to society. In a speech about trademarks Chaptal said on 17 July 1824: 'Do not tell me that in the final analysis a shopper will know about the different qualities of a material. No, gentlemen, a consumer is no judge of them; he will go only by the appearance of the commodity. But are looking and touching enough to determine the permanence of colours, the fineness of a material, or the quality and nature of its finish?' In the same measure as the expertness of a customer declines, the importance of his taste increases – both for him and for the manufacturer. For the consumer it has the value of a more or less elaborate masking of his lack of expertness. Its value to the manufacturer is a fresh stimulus to consumption which in some cases is satisfied at the expense of other requirements of consumption the manufacturer would find more costly to meet.

It is precisely this development which literature reflects in *l'art pour l'art*. This doctrine and its corresponding practice for the first time give taste a dominant position in poetry. (To be sure, taste does not seem to be the object there; it is not mentioned anywhere. But this proves no more than does the fact that taste was often discussed in the aesthetic debates of the eighteenth century. Actually, these debates centred on the content.) In *l'art pour l'art* the poet for the first time faces language the way the buyer faces the commodity on the open market. He has lost his familiarity with the process of its production to a particularly high degree. The poets of *l'art pour l'art* are the last about whom it can be said that they come 'from the people'. They have nothing to formulate with such urgency that it could determine the *coining* of their words.

Rather, they have to choose their words. The 'chosen word' soon became the motto of the *Jugendstil* literature.[2] The poet of *l'art pour l'art* wanted to bring to language above all himself – with all the idiosyncrasies, nuances, and imponderables of his nature. These elements are reflected in taste. The poet's taste guides him in his choice of words. But the choice is made only among words which have not already been coined by the *object* itself – that is, which have not been included in its process of production.

In point of fact, the theory of *l'art pour l'art* assumed decisive importance around 1852, at a time when the bourgeoisie sought to take its 'cause' from the hands of the writers and the poets. In *The Eighteenth Brumaire* Marx recollects this moment, when 'the extra-parliamentary masses of the bourgeoisie . . . through the brutal abuse of their own press', called upon Napoleon 'to destroy their speaking and writing segment, their politicians and literati, so so that they might confidently pursue their private affairs under the protection of a strong and untrammelled government'. At the end of this development may be found Mallarmé and the theory of *poésie pure*. There the cause of his own class has become so far removed from the poet that the problem of a literature without an object becomes the centre of discussion. This discussion takes place not least in Mallarmé's poems, which revolve about *blanc*, *absence*, *silence*, *vide*. This, to be sure – and particularly in Mallarmé – is the face of a coin whose other side is by no means insignificant. It furnishes evidence that the poet no longer undertakes to support any of the causes that are pursued by the class to which he belongs. To build a production on this basic renunciation of all manifest experiences of this class, causes specific and considerable difficulties. These difficulties turn this poetry into an esoteric poetry. Baudelaire's works are not esoteric. The social experiences which are reflected in his work are, to be sure, nowhere derived from the production process – least of all in its most advanced form, the industrial process – but all of them originated in extensive round-about ways. But these roundabout ways are quite apparent in his works. The most important among them are the experiences of the neurasthenic, of the big-city dweller, and of the customer.

2. 'Pierre Louys écrit: le throne: on trouve partout des abymes, des ymages, ennuy des fleurs, etc. . . . . Triomphe de l'y.'

Some Motifs in Baudelaire

I

Baudelaire envisaged readers to whom the reading of lyric poetry would present difficulties. The introductory poem of the *Fleurs du mal* is addressed to these readers. Will power and the ability to concentrate are not their strong points; what they prefer is sensual pleasures; they are familiar with the 'spleen' which kills interest and receptiveness. It is strange to come across a lyric poet who addresses himself to this, the least rewarding type of audience. There is of course a ready explanation for it. Baudelaire was anxious to be understood; he dedicates his book to kindred spirits. The poem addressed to the reader ends with the salutation: *'Hypocrite lecteur, – mon semblable, – mon frère!'*[1] It might be more fruitful to put it another way and say: Baudelaire wrote a book which from the very beginning had little prospect of becoming an immediate popular success. The kind of reader he envisaged is described in the introductory poem, and this turned out to have been a far-sighted judgment. He was eventually to find the reader at whom his work was aimed. This situation, the fact, in other words, that the climate for lyric poetry has become increasingly inhospitable, is attested to, among other things, by three factors. In the first place, the lyric poet has ceased to represent the poet *per se*. He is no longer a 'minstrel', as Lamartine still was; he has become a representative of a genre. (Verlaine is a concrete example of this specialization; Rimbaud must already be regarded as an esoteric figure, a poet who

1. Charles Baudelaire, *Oeuvres*, edited by Yves-Gérard Le Dantec, 2 vols., Paris, 1931-2, vol. I, p. 18 [henceforth cited only by volume and page number].

maintained an *ex officio* distance between his public and his work.)
Secondly, there has been no success on a mass scale in lyric poetry
since Baudelaire. (The lyric poetry of Victor Hugo was still able to
set off powerful reverberations when it first appeared. In Germany,
Heine's *Buch der Lieder* marks a watershed.) As a result, a third
factor was the greater coolness of the public even towards the lyric
poetry that had been handed down as part of its own cultural
heritage. The period in question dates back roughly to the middle
of the last century. Throughout it the fame of the *Fleurs du mal* has
constantly spread. This book, which was expected to be read by the
least indulgent of readers and which was at first read by few indulgent ones, has, over the decades, acquired the stature of a classic and
become one of the most widely printed ones as well.

If conditions for a positive reception of lyric poetry have become
less favourable, it is reasonable to assume that only in rare instances
is lyric poetry in rapport with the experience of its readers. This
may be due to a change in the structure of their experience. Even
though one may approve of this development, one may be all the
more hard put to it to say precisely in what respect there may have
been a change. Thus one turns to philosophy for an answer, which
brings one up against a strange situation. Since the end of the last
century, philosophy has made a series of attempts to lay hold of the
'true' experience as opposed to the kind that manifests itself in the
standardized, denatured life of the civilized masses. It is customary
to classify these efforts under the heading of a 'philosophy of life'.
Their point of departure, understandably enough, was not man's
life in society. What they invoked was poetry, preferably nature,
and, most recently, the age of myths. Dilthey's book *Das Erlebnis
und die Dichtung* represents one of the earliest of these efforts which
end with Klages and Jung, who made common cause with Fascism.
Towering above this literature is Bergson's early monumental
work, *Matière et mémoire*. More than the others, it preserves links
with empirical research. It is oriented towards biology. The title
suggests that it regards the structure of memory as decisive for the
philosophical pattern of experience. Experience is indeed a matter
of tradition, in collective existence as well as private life. It is less
the product of facts firmly anchored in memory than of a conver-
gence in memory of accumulated and frequently unconscious data.

It is, however, not at all Bergson's intention to attach any specific historical label to memory. On the contrary, he rejects any historical determination of memory. He thus manages above all to stay clear of that experience from which his own philosophy evolved or, rather, in reaction to which it arose. It was the inhospitable, blinding age of big-scale industrialism. In shutting out this experience the eye perceives an experience of a complementary nature in the form of its spontaneous after-image, as it were. Bergson's philosophy represents an attempt to give the details of this after-image and to fix it as a permanent record. His philosophy thus indirectly furnishes a clue to the experience which presented itself to Baudelaire's eyes in its undistorted version in the figure of his reader.

II

Matière et mémoire defines the nature of experience in the *durée* in such a way that the reader is bound to conclude that only a poet can be the adequate subject of such an experience. And it was indeed a poet who put Bergson's theory of experience to the test. Proust's work *A la recherche du temps perdu* may be regarded as an attempt to produce experience synthetically, as Bergson imagines it, under today's conditions, for there is less and less hope that it will come into being naturally. Proust, incidentally, does not evade the question in his work. He even introduces a new factor, one that involves an immanent critique of Bergson. Bergson emphasized the antagonism between the *vita activa* and the specific *vita contemplativa* which arises from memory. But he leads us to believe that turning to the contemplative actualization of the stream of life is a matter of free choice. From the start Proust indicates his divergent view terminologically. To him, the *mémoire pure* of Bergson's theory becomes a *mémoire involontaire*. Proust immediately confronts this involuntary memory with a voluntary memory, one that is in the service of the intellect. The first pages of his great work are charged with making this relationship clear. In the reflection which introduces the term Proust tells us how poorly, for many years, he remembered the town of Combray in which, after all, he spent part of his childhood. One afternoon the taste of a kind of pastry called *madeleine* (which he later mentions often) transported him back to the past, whereas before then he had been limited to the promptings of a memory which obeyed the call of attentiveness. This he calls the *mémoire volontaire*, and it is its characteristic that the information which it gives about the past retains no trace of it. 'It is the same with our own past. In vain we try to conjure it up again; the efforts of our intellect are futile.'[2] Therefore Proust, summing up, says that the past is 'somewhere beyond the reach of the intellect, and un-mistakably present in some material object (or in the sensation which such an object arouses in us), though we have no idea which one it is. As for that object, it depends entirely on chance whether we come upon it before we die or whether we never encounter it.'[3]

According to Proust, it is a matter of chance whether an indivi-dual forms an image of himself, whether he can take hold of his experience. It is by no means inevitable to be dependent on chance in this matter. Man's inner concerns do not have their issueless private character by nature. They do so only when he is increas-ingly unable to assimilate the data of the world around him by way of experience. Newspapers constitute one of many evidences of such an inability. If it were the intention of the press to have the reader assimilate the information it supplies as part of his own experience, it would not achieve its purpose. But its intention is just the oppo-site, and it is achieved: to isolate what happens from the realm in which it could affect the experience of the reader. The principles of journalistic information (freshness of the news, brevity, com-prehensibility, and, above all, lack of connection between the individual news items) contribute as much to this as does the make-up of the pages and the paper's style. (Karl Kraus never tired of demonstrating the great extent to which the linguistic usage of newspapers paralysed the imagination of their readers.) Another reason for the isolation of information from experience is that the former does not enter 'tradition'. Newspapers appear in large

2. Marcel Proust, *A la recherche du temps perdu*, vol. 1: *Du côté de chez Swann*, Paris, 1917, p. 69.
3. Proust, ibid.

editions. Few readers can boast of any information which another reader may require of him.

Historically, the various modes of communication have competed with one another. The replacement of the older narration by information, of information by sensation, reflects the increasing atrophy of experience. In turn, there is a contrast between all these forms and the story, which is one of the oldest forms of communication. It is not the object of the story to convey a happening *per se*, which is the purpose of information; rather, it embeds it in the life of the storyteller in order to pass it on as experience to those listening. It thus bears the marks of the storyteller much as the earthen vessel bears the marks of the potter's hand.

Proust's eight-volume work conveys an idea of the efforts it took to restore the figure of the storyteller to the present generation. Proust undertook this assignment with magnificent consistency. From the outset this involved him in the primary task of resurrecting his own childhood. In saying that it was a matter of chance whether the problem could be solved at all, he gave the full measure of its difficulty. In connection with these reflections he coined the phrase *mémoire involontaire.* This concept bears the marks of the situation which gave rise to it; it is part of the inventory of the individual who is isolated in many ways. Where there is experience in the strict sense of the word, certain contents of the individual past combine with material of the collective past. The rituals with their ceremonies, their festivals (quite probably nowhere recalled in Proust's work), kept producing the amalgamation of these two elements of memory over and over again. They triggered recollection at certain times and remained handles of memory for a lifetime. In this way, voluntary and involuntary recollection lose their mutual exclusiveness.

III

In seeking a more substantial definition of what appears in Proust's *mémoire de l'intelligence* as a by-product of Bergson's theory, it is well to go back to Freud. In 1921 Freud published his essay *Beyond the Pleasure Principle*, which presents a correlation between memory (in the sense of the *mémoire involontaire*) and consciousness in the form of a hypothesis. The following remarks based on it are not intended to confirm it; we shall have to content ourselves with investigating the fruitfulness of this hypothesis in situations far removed from those which Freud had in mind when he wrote. Freud's pupils are more likely to have encountered such situations. Some of Reik's writings on his own theory of memory are in line with Proust's distinction between involuntary and voluntary recollection. 'The function of remembrance [*Gedächtnis*],' Reik writes, 'is the protection of impressions; memory [*Erinnerung*] aims at their disintegration. Remembrance is essentially conservative, memory is destructive.'[4] Freud's fundamental thought, on which these remarks are based, is formulated by the assumption that 'consciousness comes into being at the site of a memory trace'.[5] (For our purposes, there is no substantial difference between the concepts *Erinnerung* and *Gedächtnis*, as used in Freud's essay.) Therefore, 'it would be the special characteristic of consciousness that, unlike what happens in all other psychical systems, the excitatory process does not leave behind a permanent change in its elements, but expires, as it were, in the phenomenon of becoming conscious'.[6] The basic formula of this hypothesis is that 'becoming conscious and leaving behind a memory trace are processes incompatible with each other within one and the same system'.[7] Rather, memory fragments are 'often most powerful and most enduring when the incident which left them behind was one that never entered consciousness'.[8] Put in Proustian terms, this means that only what has not been experienced explicitly and consciously, what has not happened to the subject as an experience, can become a component of the *mémoire involontaire*. According to Freud, the attribution of 'permanent traces as the basis of memory' to processes of stimulation is reserved for 'other systems', which must

4. Theodor Reik, *Der überraschte Psychologe. Über Erraten und Verstehen unbewusster Vorgänge*, Leiden, 1935, p. 132.

5. Sigmund Freud, *Jenseits des Lustprinzips (Beyond the Pleasure Principle)*, Vienna, 1923, p. 31.

6. Freud, ibid., pp. 31ff.   7. Freud, ibid., p. 31.

8. Freud, ibid., p. 30.

be thought of as different from consciousness.[9] In Freud's view, consciousness as such receives no memory traces whatever, but has another important function: protection against stimuli. 'For a living organism, protection against stimuli is an almost more important function than the reception of stimuli; the protective shield is equipped with its own store of energy and must above all strive to preserve the special forms of conversion of energy operating in it against the effects of the excessive energies at work in the external world, effects which tend towards an equalization of potential and hence towards destruction.'[10] The threat from these energies is one of shocks. The more readily consciousness registers these shocks, the less likely are they to have a traumatic effect. Psychoanalytic theory strives to understand the nature of these traumatic shocks 'on the basis of their breaking through the protective shield against stimuli'. According to this theory, fright has 'significance' in the 'absence of any preparedness for anxiety'.[11]

Freud's investigation was occasioned by a dream characteristic of accident neuroses which reproduce the catastrophe in which the patient was involved. Dreams of this kind, according to Freud, 'endeavour to master the stimulus retroactively, by developing the anxiety whose omission was the cause of the traumatic neurosis'.[12] Valéry seems to have had something similar in mind. The coincidence is worth noting, for Valéry was among those interested in the special functioning of psychic mechanisms under present-day conditions. (Moreover, Valéry was able to reconcile this interest with his poetic production, which remained exclusively lyric. He thus emerges as the only author who goes back directly to Baudelaire.) 'The impressions and sense perceptions of man,' Valéry writes, 'actually belong in the category of surprises; they are

9. Proust repeatedly concerns himself with these 'other systems'. Limbs are his favourite representation of them, and he frequently speaks of the memory images deposited in limbs – images that suddenly break into memory without any command from consciousness when a thigh, an arm, or a shoulder blade happen to assume a position in bed that they had at some earlier time. The *mémoire involontaire des membres* is one of Proust's favourite subjects [cf. Proust, *A la recherche du temps perdu*, vol. 1, *Du côté de chez Swann*, Paris, 1962, vol. 1, p. 6].

10. Freud, ibid., pp. 34ff.   11. Freud, ibid., p. 41.
12. Freud, ibid., p. 42.

evidence of an insufficiency in man. . . . Recollection is . . . an elemental phenomenon which aims at giving us the time for organizing the reception of stimuli which we initially lacked.'[13] The acceptance of shocks is facilitated by training in coping with stimuli, and, if need be, dreams as well as recollection may be enlisted. As a rule, however – so Freud assumes – this training devolves upon the wakeful consciousness, located in a part of the cortex which is 'so blown out by the effect of the stimulus'[14] that it offers the most favourable situation for the reception of stimuli. That the shock is thus cushioned, parried by consciousness, would lend the incident that occasions it the character of having been lived in the strict sense. If it were incorporated directly in the registry of conscious memory, it would sterilize this incident for poetic experience.

The question suggests itself how lyric poetry can have as its basis an experience for which the shock experience has become the norm. One would expect such poetry to have a large measure of consciousness; it would suggest that a plan was at work in its composition. This is indeed true of Baudelaire's poetry; it establishes a connection between him and Poe, among his predecessors, and with Valéry, among his successors. Proust's and Valéry's reflections concerning Baudelaire complement each other providentially. Proust wrote an essay about Baudelaire the significance of which is even exceeded by certain reflections in his novels. In his 'Situation de Baudelaire' Valéry supplies the classical introduction to the *Fleurs du mal.* There he says: 'The problem for Baudelaire was bound to be this: to become a great poet, yet neither Lamartine nor Hugo nor Musset. I do not claim that this ambition was a conscious one in Baudelaire; but it was bound to be present in him, it was his *raison d'état*.'[15] There is something odd about speaking of a *raison d'état* in the case of a poet; there is something remarkable about it: the emancipation from experiences. Baudelaire's poetic output is assigned a mission. He envisioned blank spaces which he filled in with his poems. His work cannot merely be categorized as historical,

13. Paul Valéry, *Oeuvres* [edited by Hytier, Paris, 1960, vol. 2, p. 741].

14. Freud, op. cit., p. 32.

15. Baudelaire, *Les Fleurs du mal*, with an Introduction by Paul Valéry, Paris, 1928.

like anyone else's, but it intended to be so and understood itself as such.

IV

The greater the share of the shock factor in particular impressions, the more constantly consciousness has to be alert as a screen against stimuli; the more efficiently it is so, the less do these impressions enter experience (*Erfahrung*), tending to remain in the sphere of a certain hour in one's life (*Erlebnis*). Perhaps the special achievement of shock defence may be seen in its function of assigning to an incident a precise point in time in consciousness at the cost of the integrity of its contents. This would be a peak achievement of the intellect; it would turn the incident into a moment that has been lived (*Erlebnis*). Without reflection there would be nothing but the sudden start, usually the sensation of fright which, according to Freud, confirms the failure of the shock defence. Baudelaire has portrayed this condition in a harsh image. He speaks of a duel in which the artist, just before being beaten, screams in fright.[16] This duel is the creative process itself. Thus Baudelaire placed the shock experience at the very centre of his artistic work. This self-portrait, which is corroborated by evidence from several contemporaries, is of great significance. Since he is himself exposed to fright, it is not unusual for Baudelaire to occasion fright. Vallès tells us about his eccentric grimaces;[17] on the basis of a portrait by Nargeot, Pontmartin establishes Baudelaire's alarming appearance; Claudel stresses the cutting quality he could give to his speech; Gautier speaks of the italicizing Baudelaire indulged in when reciting poetry;[18] Nadar describes his jerky gait.[19]

Psychiatry knows traumatophile types. Baudelaire made it his business to parry the shocks, no matter where they might come

16. Quoted in Ernest Raynaud, *Charles Baudelaire*, Paris, 1922, pp. 317ff.

17. cf. Jules Vallès, 'Charles Baudelaire', in André Billy, *Les écrivains de combat*, Paris, 1931, p. 192.

18. cf. Eugène Marsan, *Les cannes de M. Paul Bourget et le bon choix de Philinte. Petit manuel de l'homme élégant*, Paris, 1923, p. 239.

19. cf. Firmin Maillard, *La cité des intellectuels*, Paris, 1905, p. 362.

from, with his spiritual and his physical self. This shock defence is depicted graphically in an attitude of combat. Baudelaire describes his friend Constantin Guys, whom he visits when Paris is asleep: '. . . how he stands there, bent over his table, scrutinizing the sheet of paper just as intently as he does the objects around him by day; how he *stabs away* with his pencil, his pen, his brush; how he spurts water from his glass to the ceiling and tries his pen on his shirt; how he pursues his work swiftly and intensely, as though afraid that his images might escape him; thus he is combative, even when alone, and parries his own blows.'[20] In the opening stanza of his poem 'Le Soleil' Baudelaire has pictured himself engaged in such a fantastic combat; this is probably the only place in *Les Fleurs du mal* that shows the poet at work.

> Le long du vieux faubourg, où pendent aux masures
> Les persiennes, abri des secrètes luxures,
> Quand le soleil cruel frappe à traits redoublés
> Sur la ville et les champs, sur les toits et les blés,
> Je vais m'exercer seul à ma fantasque escrime,
> Flairant dans tous les coins les hasards de la rime,
> Trébuchant sur les mots comme sur les pavés,
> Heurtant parfois des vers depuis longtemps rêvés.[21]

> (Through the old suburb, where the persian blinds hang at the windows of tumbledown houses, hiding furtive pleasures; when the cruel sun strikes blow upon blow on the city and the meadows, the roofs and the cornfields, I go practising my fantastic fencing all alone, scenting a chance rhyme in every corner, stumbling against words as against cobblestones, sometimes striking on verses I had long dreamt of.)

> *translated by Francis Scarfe*

Shock is among those experiences that have assumed decisive importance for Baudelaire's personality. Gide has dealt with the interstices between image and idea, word and thing, which are the real site of Baudelaire's poetic excitation.[22] Rivière has pointed to the

20. II, 334.   21. I, 96.
22. cf. André Gide, 'Baudelaire et M. Faguet', in *Morceaux choisis*, Paris, 1921, p. 128.

subterranean shocks by which Baudelaire's poetry is shaken; it is as though they caused words to collapse. Rivière has indicated such collapsing words.[23]

> Et qui sait si les fleurs nouvelles que je rêve
> Trouveront dans ce sol lavé comme une grève
> Le mystique aliment qui *ferait* leur vigueur.[24]

> (And who knows whether my dreams' new flowers will find within this soul, washed like a shore, the mystic nourishment that would give them strength?)

Or:

> Cybèle, qui les aime, *augmente ses verdures.*[25]

> (Cybele, who loves them, augments her verdure.)

Another example is this famous first line:

> La servante au grand coeur dont vous étiez *jalouse.*[26]

> (That magnanimous servant of whom you were jealous.)

To give these covert laws their due outside his verses as well was Baudelaire's intention in his *Spleen de Paris*, his prose poems. In the dedication of his collection to the editor-in-chief of *La Presse*, Arsène Houssaye, Baudelaire wrote: 'Who among us has not dreamt, in moments of ambition, of the miracle of a poetic prose, musical without rhythm and without rhyme, supple and staccato enough to adapt to the lyrical stirrings of the soul, the undulations of dreams, and the sudden leaps of consciousness. This obsessive ideal is above all a child of the experience of giant cities, of the intersecting of their myriad relations.'[27]

This passage suggests two insights. For one thing, it tells us about the close connection in Baudelaire between the figure of shock and contact with the metropolitan masses. For another, it tells us what is really meant by these masses. They do not stand for classes or any sort of collective; rather, they are nothing but the

23. cf. Jacques Rivière, *Etudes* [Paris, 1948, p. 14].
24. I, 29.   25. I, 31.   26. I, 113.
27. I, 405ff.

amorphous crowd of passers-by, the people in the street.[28] This crowd, of whose existence Baudelaire is always aware, has not served as the model for any of his works, but it is imprinted on his creativity as a hidden figure, just as it constitutes the figure concealed in the fragment quoted before. We may discern the image of the fencer in it; the blows he deals are designed to open a path through the crowd for him. To be sure, the *faubourgs* through which the poet of 'Le Soleil' makes his way are deserted. But the meaning of the hidden configuration (which reveals the beauty of that stanza to its very depth) probably is this: it is the phantom crowd of the words, the fragments, the beginnings of lines from which the poet, in the deserted streets, wrests the poetic booty.

V

The crowd – no subject was more entitled to the attention of nineteenth-century writers. It was getting ready to take shape as a public in broad strata who had acquired facility in reading. It became a customer; it wished to find itself portrayed in the contemporary novel, as the patrons did in the paintings of the Middle Ages. The most successful author of the century met this demand out of inner necessity. To him, crowd meant – almost in the ancient sense – the crowd of the clients, the public. Victor Hugo was the first to address the crowd in his titles: *Les Misérables, Les Travailleurs de la mer*. In France, Hugo was the only writer able to compete with the serial novel. As is generally known, Eugène Sue was the master of this genre, which began to be the source of revelation for the man in the street. In 1850 an overwhelming majority elected him to Parliament as representative of the city of Paris. It is no accident that the young Marx chose Sue's *Les Mystères de Paris* for an attack. He early recognized it as his task to forge the amorphous

28. To endow this crowd with a soul is the very special purpose of the *flâneur*. His encounters with it are the experience that he does not tire of telling about. Certain reflexes of this illusion are an integral part of Baudelaire's work. It has continued to be an active force to this day. Jules Romains's *unanimisme* is an admired late flowering of it.

mass, which was then being wooed by an aesthetic socialism, into the iron of the proletariat. Engels's description of these masses in his early writings may be regarded as a prelude, however modest, to one of Marx's themes. In his book *The Condition of the Working Class in England*, Engels writes: 'A town such as London, where a man might wander for hours together without reaching the beginning of the end, without meeting the slightest hint which could lead to the inference that there is open country within reach, is a strange thing. This colossal centralization, this heaping together of two and a half millions of human beings at one point, has multiplied the power of this two and a half millions a hundredfold. . . . But the sacrifices which all this has cost become apparent later. After roaming the streets of the capital a day or two, making headway with difficulty through the human turmoil and the endless lines of vehicles, after visiting the slums of the metropolis, one realizes for the first time that these Londoners have been forced to sacrifice the best qualities of their human nature, to bring to pass all the marvels of civilization which crowd their city. . . . The very turmoil of the streets has something repulsive, something against which human nature rebels. The hundreds of thousands of all classes and ranks crowding past each other, are they not all human beings with the same qualities and powers, and with the same interest in being happy? . . . And still they crowd by one another as though they had nothing in common, nothing to do with one another, and their only agreement is the tacit one, that each keep to his own side of the pavement, so as not to delay the opposing stream of the crowd, while it occurs to no man to honour another with so much as a glance. The brutal indifference, the unfeeling isolation of each in his private interest, becomes the more repellent and offensive, the more these individuals are crowded together, within a limited space.'[29]

This description differs markedly from those to be found in minor French masters, such as Gozlan, Delvau, or Lurine. It lacks the skill and ease with which the *flâneur* moves among the crowd and which the journalist eagerly learns from him. Engels is dismayed by the crowd; he responds with a moral reaction, and an aesthetic one as

29. Friedrich Engels, *Die Lage der arbeitenden Klasse in England*, Leipzig, 1848, pp. 36ff.

well; the speed with which people rush past one another unsettles him. The charm of his description lies in the intersecting of unshakable critical integrity with an old-fashioned attitude. The writer came from a Germany that was still provincial; he may never have faced the temptation to lose himself in a stream of people. When Hegel went to Paris for the first time not long before his death, he wrote to his wife: 'When I walk through the streets, people look just as they do in Berlin; they wear the same clothes and the faces are about the same – the same aspect, but in a large crowd.'[30] To move in this crowd was natural for a Parisian. No matter how great the distance which an individual cared to keep from it, he still was coloured by it and, unlike Engels, was not able to view it from without. As regards Baudelaire, the masses were anything but external to him; indeed, it is easy to trace in his works his defensive reaction to their attraction and allure.

The masses had become so much a part of Baudelaire that it is rare to find a description of them in his works. His most important subjects are hardly ever encountered in descriptive form. As Desjardin so aptly put it, he was 'more concerned with implanting the image in the memory than with adorning and elaborating it'.[31] It is futile to search in *Les Fleurs du mal* or in *Spleen de Paris* for any counterpart to the portrayals of the city which Victor Hugo wrote with such mastery. Baudelaire describes neither the Parisians nor their city. Foregoing such descriptions enables him to invoke the one in the forms of the other. His crowd is alway the crowd of a big city, his Paris is invariably overpopulated. It is this that makes him so superior to Barbier, whose descriptive method caused a rift between the masses and the city.[32] In *Tableaux parisiens* the secret

30. Georg Wilhelm Friedrich Hegel, *Werke*, vol. 19: *Briefe von und an Hegel*, edited by Karl Hegel, Leipzig, 1887, part 2, p. 257.

31. Paul Desjardin, 'Charles Baudelaire', in *La revue bleue*, Paris, 1887, p. 23.

32. Characteristic of Barbier's method is his poem 'Londres' which in 24 lines describes the city, awkwardly closing with the following verses:

> Enfin, dans un amas de choses, sombre, immense,
> Un peuple noir, vivant et mourant en silence.
> Des êtres par milliers, suivant l'instinct fatal,
> Et courant après l'or par le bien et le mal.

presence of a crowd is demonstrable almost everywhere. When Baudelaire takes the dawn as his theme, the deserted streets emanate something of that 'silence of a throng' which Hugo senses in nocturnal Paris. As Baudelaire looks at the plates in the anatomical works for sale on the dusty banks of the Seine, the mass of the departed takes the place of the singular skeletons on these pages. In the figures of the *danse macabre*, he sees a compact mass on the move. The heroism of the wizened old women whom the cycle 'Les Petites vieilles' follows on their rounds, consists in their standing apart from the crowd, unable to keep its pace, no longer participating with their thoughts in the present. The mass was the agitated veil; through it Baudelaire saw Paris.[33] The presence of the mass

---

> (Finally, within a huge and sombre mass of things,
> A blackened people, who live and die in silence.
> Thousands of beings, who follow a fatal instinct,
> Pursuing gold with good and evil means.)

(Auguste Barbier, *Iambes et poèmes*, Paris, 1841.) Barbier's tendentious poems, particularly the London cycle, *Lazare*, influenced Baudelaire more profoundly than people have been willing to admit. Baudelaire's 'Crépuscule du soir' concludes as follows:

> ... ils finissent
> Leur destinée et vont vers le gouffre commun;
> L'hôpital se remplit de leurs soupirs. – Plus d'un
> Ne viendra plus chercher la soupe parfumée,
> Au coin du feu, le soir, auprès d'une âme aimée.

> (... their fate
> Accomplished, they approach the common pit;
> Their sighings fill the ward. – More than one
> Will come no more to get his fragrant soup,
> At night, by the fireside, next to a beloved one.)

Compare this with the end of the eighth stanza of Barbier's 'Mineurs de Newcastle':

> Et plus d'un qui rêvait dans le fond de son âme
> Aux douceurs du logis, à l'oeil bleu de sa femme,
> Trouve au ventre du gouffre un éternel tombeau.

> (And more than one who in his heart of hearts had dreams
> Of home, sweet home, and of his wife's blue eyes,
> Finds, within the belly of the pit, an everlasting tomb.)

33. Phantasmagoria, where persons who wait spend their time, a Venice

determines one of the most famous components of *Les Fleurs du mal.*

In the sonnet 'A une passante' the crowd is nowhere named in either word or phrase. And yet the whole happening hinges on it, just as the progress of a sailing-boat depends on the wind.

La rue assourdissante autour de moi hurlait.
Longue, mince, en grand deuil, douleur majestueuse,
Une femme passa, d'une main fastueuse
Soulevant, balançant le feston et l'ourlet;

Agile et noble, avec sa jambe de statue.
Moi, je buvais, crispé comme un extravagant,
Dans son oeil, ciel livide où germe l'ouragan,
La douceur qui fascine et le plaisir qui tue.

Un éclair . . . puis la nuit! – Fugitive beauté
Dont le regard m'a fait soudainement renaître,
Ne te verrai-je plus que dans l'éternité?

Ailleurs, bien loin d'ici! Trop tard! *jamais* peut-être!
Car j'ignore où tu fuis, tu ne sais où je vais,
O toi que j'eusse aimée, ô toi qui le savais![34]

(Amid the deafening traffic of the town,
Tall, slender, in deep mourning, with majesty,
A woman passed, raising, with dignity
In her poised hand, the flounces of her gown;

Graceful, noble, with a statue's form.
And I drank, trembling as a madman thrills,
From her eyes, ashen sky where brooded storm,
The softness that fascinates, the pleasure that kills.

A flash . . . then night! – O lovely fugitive,
I am suddenly reborn from your swift glance;
Shall I never see you till eternity?

---

composed of arcades and presented by the Empire to Parisians, as a dream, transports only a few on its mosaic conveyor-belt. This is why there are no arcades in Baudelaire.

34. I, 106.

Somewhere, far off! too late! *never*, perchance!
Neither knows where the other goes or lives;
We might have loved, and you knew this might be!)

translated by C. F. MacIntyre

In a widow's veil, mysteriously and mutely borne along by the crowd, an unknown woman comes into the poet's field of vision. What this sonnet communicates is simply this: far from experiencing the crowd as an opposed, antagonistic element, this very crowd brings to the city dweller the figure that fascinates. The delight of the urban poet is love – not at first sight, but at last sight. It is a farewell forever which coincides in the poem with the moment of enchantment. Thus the sonnet supplies the figure of shock, indeed of catastrophe. But the nature of the poet's emotions has been affected as well. What makes his body contract in a tremor – *crispé comme un extravagant*, Baudelaire says – is not the rapture of a man whose every fibre is suffused with *eros*; it is, rather, like the kind of sexual shock that can beset a lonely man. The fact that 'these verses could only have been written in a big city',[35] as Thibaudet put it, is not very meaningful. They reveal the stigmata which life in a metropolis inflicts upon love. Proust read the sonnet in this light, and that is why he gave his later echo of the woman in mourning, which appeared to him one day in the form of Albertine, the evocative caption 'La Parisienne'. 'When Albertine came into my room again, she wore a black satin dress. It made her pale, and she resembled the type of the fiery and yet pale Parisian woman, the woman who is not used to fresh air and has been affected by living among masses and possibly in an atmosphere of vice, the kind that can be recognized by a certain glance which seems unsteady if there is no rouge on her cheeks.'[36] This is the look – even as late as Proust – of the object of a love which only a city dweller experiences, which Baudelaire captured for poetry, and of which one might not infrequently say that it was spared, rather than denied, fulfilment.[37]

35. Albert Thibaudet, *Intérieurs*, Paris, 1924, p. 22.
36. Proust, *A la recherche du temps perdu*, vol. 6: *La Prisonnière*, Paris, 1923, p. 138.
37. The motif of love for a woman passing by occurs in an early poem by Stefan George. The poet has missed the important thing: the stream in which

VI

A story by Poe which Baudelaire translated may be
regarded as the classic example among the older versions of the
motif of the crowd. It is marked by certain peculiarities which, upon
closer inspection, reveal aspects of social forces of such power and
hidden depth that we may count them among those which alone are
capable of exerting both a subtle and a profound effect upon artistic
production. The story is entitled 'The Man of the Crowd'. Set in
London, its narrator is a man who, after a long illness, ventures out
again for the first time into the hustle and bustle of the city. In the
late afternoon hours of an autumn day he installs himself behind a
window in a big London coffee-house. He looks over the other
guests, pores over advertisements in the paper, but his main focus
of interest is the throng of people surging past his window in the
street. 'The latter is one of the principal thoroughfares of the city,
and had been very much crowded during the whole day. But, as the
darkness came on, the throng momently increased; and by the time
the lamps were well lighted, two dense and continuous tides of
population were rushing past the door. At this particular period of
the evening I had never before been in a similar situation, and the
tumultuous sea of human heads filled me, therefore, with a delicious
novelty of emotion. I gave up, at length, all care of things within the
hotel, and became absorbed in contemplation of the scene without.'
Important as it is, let us disregard the narrative to which this is the
prelude and examine the setting.

The appearance of the London crowd as Poe describes it is as
gloomy and fitful as the light of the gas lamps overhead. This applies
not only to the riffraff that is 'brought forth, from its den' as night

---

the woman moves past, borne along by the crowd. The result is a self-
conscious elegy. The poet's glances – so he must confess to his lady – have
'moved away, moist with longing/before they dared mingle with yours'
('. . . *feucht vor sehnen fortgezogen/eh sie in deine sich zu tauchen trauten.*' Stefan
George, *Hymnen. Pilgerfahrten. Algabal*, Berlin, 1922). Baudelaire leaves no
doubt that *he* looked deep into the eyes of the passer-by.

falls. The employees of higher rank, 'the upper clerks of staunch firms', Poe describes as follows: 'They had all slightly bald heads, from which the right ears, long used to pen-holding, had an odd habit of standing off on end. I observed that they always removed or settled their hats with both hands, and wore watches, with short gold chains of a substantial and ancient pattern.' Even more striking is his description of the crowd's movements. 'By far the greater number of those who went by had a satisfied business-like demeanour, and seemed to be thinking only of making their way through the press. Their brows were knit, and their eyes rolled quickly; when pushed against by fellow-wayfarers they evinced no symptom of impatience, but adjusted their clothes and hurried on. Others, still a numerous class, were restless in their movements, had flushed faces, and talked and gesticulated to themselves, as if feeling in solitude on account of the very denseness of the company around. When impeded in their progress, these people suddenly ceased muttering, but redoubled their gesticulations, and awaited, with an absent and overdone smile upon the lips, the course of the persons impeding them. If jostled, they bowed profusely to the jostlers, and appeared overwhelmed with confusion.'[38] One might think he was

---

38. This passage has a parallel in 'Un Jour de pluie.' Even though it bears another name, this poem must be ascribed to Baudelaire. The last verse, which gives the poem its extraordinarily sombre quality, has an exact counterpart in 'The Man of the Crowd'. Poe writes: 'The rays of the gas lamps, feeble at first in their struggle with the dying day, had now at length gained ascendancy, and threw over everything a fitful and garish lustre. All was dark yet splendid – as that ebony to which has been likened the style of Tertullian.' This coincidence is all the more astonishing here as the following verses were written in 1843 at the latest, a period when Baudelaire did not know Poe.

> Chacun, nous coudoyant sur le trottoir glissant,
> Egoïste et brutal, passe et nous éclabousse,
> Ou, pour courir plus vite, en s'éloignant nous pousse.
> Partout fange, déluge, obscurité du ciel:
> Noir tableau qu'eût rêvé le noir Ezéchiel!

> (Each one, elbowing us upon the slippery sidewalk,
> Selfish and savage, goes by and splashes us,
> Or, to run the faster, gives us a push as he makes off.
> Mud everywhere, deluge, darkness in the sky.
> A sombre scene that Ezekiel the sombre might have dreamed.)

speaking of half-drunken wretches. Actually, they were 'noblemen, merchants, attorneys, tradesmen, stock-jobbers'.[39]

Poe's manner of presentation cannot be called realism. It shows a purposely distorting imagination at work, one that removes the text far from what is commonly advocated as the model of social realism. Barbier, perhaps one of the best examples of this type of realism that come to mind, describes things in a less eccentric way. Moreover, he chose a more transparent subject: the oppressed masses. Poe is not concerned with these; he deals with 'people', pure and simple. For him, as for Engels, there was something menacing in the spectacle they presented. It is precisely this image of big-city crowds that became decisive for Baudelaire. If he succumbed to the force by which he was drawn to them and, as a *flâneur*, was made one of them, he was nevertheless unable to rid himself of a sense of their essentially inhuman make-up. He becomes their accomplice even as he dissociates himself from them. He becomes deeply involved with them, only to relegate them to oblivion with a single glance of contempt. There is something compelling about this ambivalence where he cautiously admits to it. Perhaps the charm of his 'Crépuscule du soir', so difficult to account for, is bound up with this.

VII

Baudelaire saw fit to equate the man of the crowd, whom Poe's narrator follows throughout the length and breadth of nocturnal London, with the *flâneur*.[40] It is hard to accept this view. The man of the crowd is no *flâneur*. In him, composure has given way to manic behaviour. Hence he exemplifies, rather, what had to become of the *flâneur* once he was deprived of the milieu to which

39. There is something demonic about Poe's businessmen. One is reminded of Marx, who blamed the 'feverishly youthful pace of material production' in the United States for the lack of 'either time or opportunity . . . to abolish the spirit world'. As darkness descends, Baudelaire has 'the harmful demons' awaken in the air 'sluggish as a bunch of businessmen'. This passage in 'Crépuscule du soir' may have been inspired by Poe's text.

40. cf. II, 328–35.

he belonged. If London ever provided it for him, it was certainly not the setting described by Poe. In comparison, Baudelaire's Paris preserved some features that dated back to the happy old days. Ferries were still crossing the Seine at points that would later be spanned by the arch of a bridge. In the year of Baudelaire's death it was still possible for some entrepreneur to cater to the comfort of the well-to-do with a fleet of five hundred sedan chairs circulating about the city. Arcades where the *flâneur* would not be exposed to the sight of carriages that did not recognize pedestrians as rivals were enjoying undiminished popularity.[41] There was the pedestrian who would let himself be jostled by the crowd, but there was also the *flâneur* who demanded elbow room and was unwilling to forego the life of a gentleman of leisure. Let the many attend to their daily affairs; the man of leisure can indulge in the perambulations of the *flâneur* only if as such he is already out of place. He is as much out of place in an atmosphere of complete leisure as in the feverish turmoil of the city. London has its man of the crowd. His counterpart, as it were, is the boy Nante [Ferdinand], of the street corner, a popular figure in Berlin before the March Revolution of 1848; the Parisian *flâneur* might be said to stand midway between them.[42]

How the man of leisure looks upon the crowd is revealed in a short piece by E. T. A. Hoffmann, the last that he wrote, entitled 'The Cousin's Corner Window'. It antedates Poe's story by fifteen years and is probably one of the earliest attempts to capture the street scene of a large city. The differences between the two pieces are worth noting. Poe's narrator observes from behind the window of a public coffee-house, whereas the cousin is installed at home. Poe's observer succumbs to the fascination of the scene, which finally lures him outside into the whirl of the crowd. Hoffmann's

41. A pedestrian knew how to display his nonchalance provocatively on certain occasions. Around 1840 it was briefly fashionable to take turtles for a walk in the arcades. The *flâneurs* liked to have the turtles set the pace for them. If they had had their way, progress would have been obliged to accommodate itself to this pace. But this attitude did not prevail; Taylor, who popularized the watchword 'Down with dawdling!' carried the day.

42. In Glassbrenner's character the man of leisure appears as a paltry scion of the *citoyen*. Nante, Berlin's street-corner boy, has no reason to bestir himself. He makes himself at home on the street, which naturally does not lead him anywhere, and is as comfortable as the philistine is in his four walls.

cousin, looking out from his corner window, is immobilized as a paralytic; he would not be able to follow the crowd even if he were in the midst of it. His attitude towards the crowd is, rather, one of superiority, inspired as it is by his observation post at the window of an apartment building. From this vantage point he scrutinizes the throng; it is market day, and they all feel in their element. His opera glasses enable him to pick out individual genre scenes. The employment of this instrument is thoroughly in keeping with the inner disposition of its user. He would like, as he admits,[43] to initiate his visitor into the 'principles of the art of seeing'.[44] This consists of an ability to enjoy *tableaux vivants* – a favourite pursuit of the Biedermeier period. Edifying sayings provide the interpretation.[45] One can look upon the narrative as an attempt which was then due to be made. But it is obvious that the conditions under which it was made in Berlin prevented it from being a complete success. If Hoffmann had ever set foot in Paris or London, or if he had been intent upon depicting the masses as such, he would not have focused on a market place; he would not have portrayed the scene as being dominated by women; he would perhaps have seized on the motifs that Poe derives from the swarming crowds under the

43. E. T. A. Hoffmann, *Ausgewählte Schriften*, vol. 14: *Leben und Nachlass* by Julius Eduard Hitzig, vol. 2, Stuttgart, 1839, p. 205.

44. What leads up to this confession is remarkable. The visitor says that the cousin watches the bustle down below only because he enjoys the changing play of the colours; in the long run, he says, this must be tiring. In a similar vein, and probably not much later, Gogol wrote of a fair in the Ukraine: 'So many people were on their way there that it made one's eyes swim.' The daily sight of a lively crowd may once have constituted a spectacle to which one's eyes had to adapt first. On the basis of this supposition, one may assume that once the eyes had mastered this task they welcomed opportunities to test their newly acquired faculties. This would mean that the technique of Impressionist painting, whereby the picture is garnered in a riot of dabs of colour, would be a reflection of experiences with which the eyes of a big-city dweller have become familiar. A picture like Monet's 'Cathedral of Chartres', which is like an ant-heap of stone, would be an illustration of this hypothesis.

45. In his story E. T. A. Hoffmann devotes edifying reflections, for instance, to the blind man who lifts his head towards the sky. In the last line of 'Les Aveugles', Baudelaire, who knew this story, modifies Hoffmann's reflections in such a way as to disprove their edifying quality: '*Que cherchent-ils au Ciel, tous ces aveugles?*' (What are all those blind people looking for in the sky?).

gas lamps. Actually, there would have been no need for these motifs in order to bring out the uncanny elements that other students of the physiognomy of the big city have felt. A thoughtful observation by Heine is relevant here: 'Heine's eyesight,' wrote a correspondent in a letter to Varnhagen in 1838, 'caused him acute trouble in the spring. On the last such occasion I was walking down one of the boulevards with him. The magnificence, the life, of this in its way unique thoroughfare roused me to boundless admiration, something that prompted Heine this time to make a significant point in stressing the horror with which this centre of the world was tinged.'[46]

VIII

Fear, revulsion, and horror were the emotions which the big-city crowd aroused in those who first observed it. For Poe it has something barbaric; discipline just barely manages to tame it. Later, James Ensor tirelessly confronted its discipline with its wildness; he liked to put military groups in his carnival mobs, and both got along splendidly – as the prototype of totalitarian states, in which the police make common cause with the looters. Valéry, who had a fine eye for the cluster of symptoms called 'civilization', has characterized one of the pertinent facts. 'The inhabitant of the great urban centres,' he writes, 'reverts to a state of savagery – that is, of isolation. The feeling of being dependent on others, which used to be kept alive by need, is gradually blunted in the smooth functioning of the social mechanism. Any improvement of this mechanism eliminates certain modes of behaviour and emotions.'[47] Comfort isolates; on the other hand, it brings those enjoying it closer to mechanization. The invention of the match around the middle of the nineteenth century brought forth a number of innovations which have one thing in common: one abrupt movement of the hand triggers a process of many steps. This development is taking place in many areas. One case in point is the telephone, where the

---

46. Heinrich Heine, *Gespräche, Briefe, Tagebücher, Berichte seiner Zeitgenossen*, collected and edited by Hugo Bieber, Berlin, 1926, p. 163.

47. Valéry, *Oeuvres*, op. cit., p. 588.

lifting of a receiver has taken the place of the steady movement that used to be required to crank the older models. Of the countless movements of switching, inserting, pressing, and the like, the 'snapping' of the photographer has had the greatest consequences. A touch of the finger now sufficed to fix an event for an unlimited period of time. The camera gave the moment a posthumous shock, as it were. Tactile experiences of this kind were joined by optic ones, such as are supplied by the advertising pages of a newspaper or the traffic of a big city. Moving through this traffic involves the individual in a series of shocks and collisions. At dangerous crossings, nervous impulses flow through him in rapid succession, like the energy from a battery. Baudelaire speaks of a man who plunges into the crowd as into a reservoir of electric energy. Circumscribing the experience of the shock, he calls this man 'a *kaleidoscope* equipped with consciousness'.[48] Whereas Poe's passers-by cast glances in all directions which still appeared to be aimless, today's pedestrians are obliged to do so in order to keep abreast of traffic signals. Thus technology has subjected the human sensorium to a complex kind of training. There came a day when a new and urgent need for stimuli was met by the film. In a film, perception in the form of shocks was established as a formal principle. That which determines the rhythm of production on a conveyor belt is the basis of the rhythm of reception in the film.

Marx had good reason to stress the great fluidity of the connection between segments in manual labour. This connection appears to the factory worker on an assembly line in an independent, reified form. Independently of the worker's volition, the article being worked on comes within his range of action and moves away from him just as arbitrarily. 'Every kind of capitalist production . . . has this in common,' wrote Marx, 'that it is not the workman that employs the instruments of labour, but the instruments of labour that employ the workman. But it is only in the factory system that this inversion for the first time acquires technical and palpable reality.'[49] In working with machines, workers learn to coordinate their own 'movements to the uniform and unceasing motion of an

48. II, 333.
49. Karl Marx, *Das Kapital*, edited by Karl Korsch, Berlin, 1932, p. 404 [English edition, *Capital*, vol. 1, London, 1967, p. 423].

automaton'.[50] These words shed a peculiar light on the absurd kind of uniformity with which Poe wants to saddle the crowd – uniformities of attire and behaviour, but also a uniformity of facial expression. Those smiles provide food for thought. They are probably the familiar kind, as expressed in the phrase 'keep smiling'; in that context they function as a mimetic shock absorber. 'All machine work,' it is said in the above context, 'requires early drilling of the workers.'[51] This drill must be differentiated from practice. Practice, which was the sole determinant in craftsmanship, still had a function in manufacturing. With it as the basis, 'each particular area of production finds its appropriate technical form in *experience* and *slowly* perfects it'. To be sure, it quickly crystallizes it, 'as soon as a certain degree of maturity has been attained'.[52] On the other hand, this same manufacturing produces, 'in every handicraft that it seizes upon, a class of so-called unskilled labourers, a class which handicraft industry strictly excluded. If it develops a one-sided speciality into a perfection, at the expense of the whole of a man's working capacity, it also begins to make a speciality of the absence of all development. Along the side of hierarchic gradation there steps the simple separation of the labourers into skilled and un-skilled.'[53] The unskilled worker is the one most deeply degraded by the drill of the machines. His work has been sealed off from experience; practice counts for nothing there.[54] What the fun fair achieves with its dodgem cars and other similar amusements is nothing but a taste of the drill to which the unskilled labourer is subjected in the factory – a sample which at times was for him the entire menu; for the art of being a clown, in which the little man could acquire training in places like the fun fair, flourished con-comitantly with unemployment. Poe's text makes us understand the true connection between wildness and discipline. His pedestrians act as if they had adapted themselves to the machines and could express

50. Marx, ibid., p. 402 [English edition, p. 421].

51. Marx, ibid.   52. Marx, ibid.

53. Marx, ibid., pp. 336ff. [English edition, p. 350].

54. The shorter the training period of an industrial worker is, the longer that of a military man becomes. It may be part of society's preparation for total war that training is shifting from the practice of production to the prac-tice of destruction.

themselves only automatically. Their behaviour is a reaction to shocks. 'If jostled, they bowed profusely to the jostlers.'

IX

The shock experience which the passer-by has in the crowd corresponds to what the worker 'experiences' at his machine. This does not entitle us to the assumption that Poe knew anything about industrial work processes. Baudelaire, at any rate, did not have the faintest notion of them. He was, however, captivated by a process whereby the reflecting mechanism which the machine sets off in the workman can be studied closely, as in a mirror, in the idler. If we say that this process is the game of chance, the statement may appear to be paradoxical. Where would one find a more evident contrast than the one between work and gambling? Alain puts it convincingly when he writes: 'It is inherent in the concept of gambling . . . that no game is dependent on the preceding one. Gambling cares about no assured position. . . . Winnings secured earlier are not taken into account, and in this it differs from work. Gambling gives short shrift to the weighty past on which work bases itself.'[55] The work which Alain has in mind here is the highly specialized kind (which, like intellectual effort, probably retains certain features of handicraft); it is not that of most factory workers, least of all the work of the unskilled. The latter, to be sure, lacks any touch of adventure, of the mirage that lures the gambler. But it certainly does not lack the futility, the emptiness, the inability to complete something which is inherent in the activity of a wage slave in a factory. Gambling even contains the workmen's gesture that is produced by the automatic operation, for there can be no game without the quick movement of the hand by which the stake is put down or a card is picked up. The jolt in the movement of a machine is like the so-called *coup* in a game of chance. The manipulation of the worker at the machine has no connection with the preceding operation for the very reason that it is its exact repetition. Since each operation at the machine is just as screened off from the

55. Alain, *Les idées et les âges*, Paris, 1927, vol. 1, pp. 183ff. ('Le jeu').

preceding operation as a *coup* in a game of chance is from the one that preceded it, the drudgery of the labourer is, in its own way, a counterpart to the drudgery of the gambler. The work of both is equally devoid of substance.

There is a lithograph by Senefelder which represents a gambling club. Not one of those depicted is pursuing the game in the customary fashion. Each man is dominated by an emotion: one shows unrestrained joy; another, distrust of his partner; a third, dull despair; a fourth evinces belligerence; another is getting ready to depart from the world. All these modes of conduct share a concealed characteristic: the figures presented show us how the mechanism to which the participants in a game of chance entrust themselves seizes them body and soul, so that even in their private sphere, and no matter how agitated they may be, they are capable only of a reflex action. They behave like the pedestrians in Poe's story. They live their lives as automatons and resemble Bergson's fictitious characters who have completely liquidated their memories.

Baudelaire does not appear to have been a devotee of gambling, although he had words of friendly understanding, even homage, for those addicted to it.[56] The motif which he treated in his night piece 'Le Jeu' was part of his view of modern times, and he considered it as part of his mission to write this poem. The image of the gambler became in Baudelaire the characteristically modern complement to the archaic image of the fencer; both are heroic figures to him. Ludwig Börne looked at things through Baudelaire's eyes when he wrote: 'If all the energy and passion . . . that are expended every year at Europe's gambling tables . . . were saved, they would suffice to fashion a Roman people and a Roman history from them. But that is just it. Because every man is born a Roman, bourgeois society seeks to de-Romanize him, and that is why there are games of chance and parlour games, novels, Italian operas, and fashionable newspapers.'[57] Gambling became a stock diversion of the bourgeoisie only in the nineteenth century; in the eighteenth, only the aristocracy gambled. Games of chance were disseminated by the Napoleonic armies, and they now became part of 'fashionable living

56. cf. I, 456 and II, 630.

57. Ludwig Börne, *Gesammelte Schriften*, Hamburg and Frankfurt, 1862, pp. 38ff.

and the thousands of unsettled lives that are lived in the basements of a large city', part of the spectacle in which Baudelaire claimed he saw the heroic – 'as it is characteristic of our epoch'.[58]

If one wants to examine gambling from the psychological as well as the technical point of view, Baudelaire's conception of it appears even more significant. It is obvious that the gambler is out to win. Yet one will not want to call his desire to win and make money a wish in the strict sense of the word. He may be inwardly motivated by greed or by some sinister determination. At any rate, his frame of mind is such that he cannot make much use of experience.[59] A wish, however, is a kind of experience. 'What one wishes for in one's youth, one has in abundance in old age,' said Goethe. The earlier in life one makes a wish, the greater one's chances that it will be fulfilled. The further a wish reaches out in time, the greater the hopes for its fulfilment. But it is experience that accompanies one to the far reaches of time, that fills and divides time. Thus a wish fulfilled is the crowning of experience. In folk symbolism, distance in space can take the place of distance in time; that is why the shooting star, which plunges into the infinite distance of space, has become the symbol of a fulfilled wish. The ivory ball which rolls into the *next* compartment, the *next* card which lies on top are the very antithesis of a falling star. The period of time encompassed by the instant in which the light of a shooting star flashes for a man is of the kind that Joubert has described with his customary assurance. 'Time,' he says, 'is found even in eternity; but it is not earthly, worldly time. . . . That time does not destroy; it merely completes.'[60] It is the antithesis of time in hell, the province of those who are not

58. II, 135.

59. Gambling invalidates the standards of experience. It may be due to an obscure sense of this that the 'vulgar appeal to experience' (Kant) has particular currency among gamblers. A gambler says 'my number' in the same way as a man about town says 'my type'. Towards the end of the Second Empire this attitude prevailed. 'On the boulevards it was customary to attribute everything to chance.' This disposition is promoted by betting, which is a device for giving events the character of a shock, detaching them from the context of experience. For the bourgeoisie, even political events were apt to assume the form of occurrences at the gambling table.

60. Joseph Joubert, *Pensées précédées de sa correspondance*, vol. 2, Paris, 1883, p. 162.

allowed to complete anything they have started. The disrepute of games of chance is actually based on the fact that the player himself has a hand in it. (An incorrigible patron of a lottery will not be proscribed in the same way as the gambler in a stricter sense.)

This starting all over again is the regulative idea of the game, as it is of work for wages. Thus it is highly meaningful if in Baudelaire the second-hand – 'la Seconde' – appears as partner of the gambler:

> *Souviens-toi* que le Temps est un joueur avide
> Qui gagne sans tricher, à tout coup! c'est la loi![61]

> (Keep in mind that Time's a rabid gambler who wins
> always without cheating – it's the law!)

In another place, Satan himself takes the place of this second.[62] The taciturn corner of the cave to which the poem 'Le Jeu' relegates those who are addicted to gambling undoubtedly is part of his realm.

> Voilà le noir tableau qu'en un rêve nocturne
> Je vis se dérouler sous mon oeil clairvoyant,
> Moi-même, dans un coin de l'antre taciturne,
> Je me vis accoudé, froid, muet enviant,
> Enviant de ces gens la passion tenace.[63]

> (Here you see the hellish picture that one night in a dream
> I saw unfolding before my clairvoyant eyes;
> And, over in a corner of this silent cave,
> Myself I saw, hunched up, cold, mute, and envying,
> Envying these people their tenacious passion.)

The poet does not participate in the game. He stands in his corner, no happier than those who are playing. He too has been cheated out of his experience – a modern man. The only difference is that he rejects the narcotics with which the gamblers seek to submerge the consciousness that has delivered them to the march of the second-hand.[64]

61. I, 49.   62. cf. I, 455–9.   63. I, 110.
64. The narcotic effect that is involved here is specified as to time, like the malady that it is supposed to alleviate. Time is the material into which the phantasmagoria of gambling has been woven. In his *Faucheurs de nuits*

Et mon coeur s'effraya d'envier maint pauvre homme
Courant avec ferveur à l'abîme béant,
Et qui, soûl de son sang, préférerait en somme
La douleur à la mort et l'enfer au néant![65]

(And my heart took fright – to envy some poor man
Who ran in frenzy to the sheer abyss,
Who, drunk with the pulsing of his blood, preferred
Grief to death, and hell to nothingness.)

In this last stanza Baudelaire presents impatience as the substratum of the passion for gambling. He found it in himself in its purest form. His violent temper had the expressiveness of Giotto's *Iracundia* at Padua.

X

It is – if one follows Bergson – the actualization of the *durée* which rids man's soul of obsession with time. Proust shared this belief, and from it he developed the lifelong exercises in which he strove to bring to light past things saturated with all the reminiscences that had worked their way into his pores during his sojourn in the unconscious. Proust was an incomparable reader of the *Fleurs du mal*, for he sensed that it contained kindred elements. Familiarity

---

Gourdon de Genouillac writes: 'I claim that the mania for gambling is the noblest of all passions, for it includes all the others. A series of lucky *coups* gives me more pleasure than a non-gambler can have in years. . . . If you think that I see only profit in the gold that falls to my share, you are mistaken. I see in it the pleasures that it gets me, and I enjoy them fully. They come too quickly to make me weary, and there are too many of them for me to get bored. I live a hundred lives in one. When I travel, it is the way that an electric spark travels. . . . If I am stingy and reserve my bank notes for gambling, it it because I know the value of time too well to invest them as other people do. A certain enjoyment that I might permit myself would cost me a thousand other enjoyments. . . . I have intellectual pleasures and want no others.' In the fine notes on gambling in his *Jardin d'Épicure*, Anatole France presents a similar view.

65. I, 110.

with Baudelaire must include Proust's experience with him. Proust writes: 'Time is peculiarly chopped up in Baudelaire; only a very few days open up, they are significant ones. Thus it is understandable why turns of phrase like "one evening" occur frequently in his works.'[66] These significant days are days of completing time, to paraphrase Joubert. They are days of recollection, not marked by any experience. They are not connected with the other days, but stand out from time. As for their substance, Baudelaire has defined it in the notion of the *correspondances*, a concept that in Baudelaire stands side by side and unconnected with the notion of 'modern beauty'.

Disregarding the scholarly literature on the *correspondances* (the common property of the mystics; Baudelaire encountered them in Fourier's writings), Proust no longer fusses about the artistic variations on the situation which are supplied by synaesthesia. The important thing is that the *correspondances* record a concept of experience which includes ritual elements. Only by appropriating these elements was Baudelaire able to fathom the full meaning of the breakdown which he, a modern man, was witnessing. Only in this way was he able to recognize in it the challenge meant for him alone, a challenge which he incorporated in the *Fleurs du mal*. If there really is a secret architecture in this book – and many speculations have been devoted to it – the cycle of poems that opens the volume probably is devoted to something irretrievably lost. This cycle includes two sonnets whose motif is the same. The first, entitled 'Correspondances', begins with these lines:

> La Nature est un temple où de vivants piliers
> Laissent parfois sortir de confuses paroles;
> L'homme y passe à travers des forêts de symboles
> Qui l'observent avec des regards familiers.
>
> Comme de longs échos qui de loin se confondent
> Dans une ténébreuse et profonde unité,
> Vaste comme la nuit et comme la clarté,
> Les parfums, les couleurs et les sons se répondent.[67]

66. Proust, 'A propos de Baudelaire', in *Nouvelle revue française*, no. 16, 1 June 1921, p. 652.

67. I, 23.

> (Nature is a temple whose living pillars
> Sometimes give forth a babel of words;
> Man wends his way through forests of symbols
> Which look at him with their familiar glances.
>
> As long-resounding echoes from afar
> Are mingling in a deep, dark unity,
> Vast as the night or as the orb of day,
> Perfumes, colours, and sounds commingle.)

What Baudelaire meant by *correspondances* may be described as an experience which seeks to establish itself in crisis-proof form. This is possible only within the realm of the ritual. If it transcends this realm, it presents itself as the beautiful. In the beautiful the ritual value of art appears.[68]

68. Beauty can be defined in two ways: in its relationship to history and to nature. In both relationships the semblance, the problematic element in the beautiful, manifests itself. (Let us indicate the first relationship briefly. On the basis of its *historical* existence, beauty is an appeal to join those who admired it at an earlier time. Being moved by beauty is an *ad plures ire*, as the Romans called dying. According to this definition, the semblance of beauty means that the identical object which admiration is courting cannot be found in the work. This admiration harvests what earlier generations have admired in it. Words of Goethe express here the final conclusion of wisdom: 'Everything that has had a great effect can really no longer be evaluated.') Beauty in its relationship to *nature* can be defined as that which 'remains true to its essential nature only when veiled'. The *correspondances* tell us what is meant by such a veil. We may call it, in a somewhat daring abbreviation, the 'reproducing aspect' of the work of art. The *correspondances* constitute the court of judgment before which the object of art is found to be a faithful reproduction – which, to be sure, makes it entirely problematic. If one attempted to reproduce this *aporia* through language, one would define beauty as the object of experience in the state of resemblance. This definition would probably coincide with Valéry's formulation: 'Beauty may require the servile imitation of what is indefinable in objects.' If Proust so readily returns to this subject (which in his work appears as time recovered), one cannot say that he is telling any secrets. It is, rather, one of the disconcerting features of his technique that he repeatedly and loquaciously builds his reflections around the concept of beauty – in short, the hermetic aspect of art. He writes about the origin and the intentions of his work with a fluency and an urbanity that would befit a refined amateur. This, to be sure, has its counterpart in Bergson. The following passage in which the philosopher indicates all the things that may be expected from a visual actualization of the uninterrupted stream of becoming has a flavour

The *correspondances* are the data of remembrance – not historical data, but data of prehistory. What makes festive days great and significant is the encounter with an earlier life. Baudelaire recorded this in a sonnet entitled 'La Vie antérieure'. The images of caves and vegetation, of clouds and waves which are evoked at the beginning of this second sonnet rise from the warm vapour of tears, tears of homesickness. 'The wanderer looks into the tear-veiled distance. and hysterical tears [*sic*] well up in his eyes,' writes Baudelaire in his review of the poems of Marceline Desbordes-Valmore.[69] There are no simultaneous correspondences, such as were cultivated by the symbolists later. The murmur of the past may be heard in the correspondences, and the canonical experience of them has its place in a previous life:

> Les houles, en roulant les images des cieux,
> Mêlaient d'une façon solennelle et mystique
> Les tout-puissants accords de leur riche musique
> Aux couleurs du couchant reflété par mes yeux.
>
> C'est là que j'ai vécu. . . .[70]
>
> (The breakers, rolling the images of the sky,
> Mixed, in a mystical and solemn way,
> The powerful chords of their rich music
> With the colours of the sunset reflected in my eyes.
>
> There did I live. . . .)

The fact that Proust's restorative will remains within the limits of earthly existence, whereas Baudelaire's transcends it, may be regarded as symptomatic of the incomparably more elemental and powerful counterforces that Baudelaire faced. And probably he nowhere achieved greater perfection than when he seems resigned

---

reminiscent of Proust. 'We can let our day-to-day existence be permeated with such a visualization and thus, thanks to philosophy, enjoy a satisfaction similar to that of art; but this satisfaction would be more frequent, more regular, and more easily accessible to ordinary mortals.' Bergson sees within reach what Valéry's better, Goethean understanding visualizes as the 'here' in which the inadequate becomes an actuality.

69. II, 536.   70. I, 30.

to being overcome by them. 'Recueillement' traces the allegories of the old years against the deep sky:

> . . . Vois se pencher les défuntes Années,
> Sur les balcons du ciel, en robes surannées.[71]
>
> (. . . See the dead departed Years in antiquated
> Dress leaning over heaven's balconies.)

In these verses Baudelaire resigns himself to paying homage to times out of mind that escaped him in the guise of the outdated. When Proust in the last volume of his work reverts to the sensation that suffused him at the taste of a *madeleine*, he imagines the years which appear on the balcony as being loving sisters of the years of Combray. 'In Baudelaire . . . these reminiscences are even more numerous. It is apparent that they are not occasioned by chance, and this, to my mind, is what gives them crucial importance. There is no one else who pursues the interconnected *correspondances* with such leisurely care, fastidiously and yet nonchalantly – in a woman's smell, for instance, in the fragrance of her hair or her breasts – *correspondances* which then yield him lines like "the azure of the vast, vaulted sky" or "a harbour full of flames and masts".'[72] These words are a confessional motto for Proust's work. It bears a relationship to Baudelaire's work, which has assembled the days of remembrance into a spiritual year.

But the *Fleurs du mal* would not be what it is if all it contained were this success. It is unique because it was able to wrest from the inefficacy of the same consolation, the breakdown of the same fervour, the failure of the same effort, poems that are in no way inferior to those in which the *correspondances* celebrate their triumphs. *Spleen et idéal* is the first of the cycles in *Les Fleurs du mal*. The *idéal* supplies the power of remembrance; the *spleen* musters the multitude of the seconds against it. It is their commander, just as the devil is the lord of the flies. One of the *Spleen* poems, 'Le Goût du néant', says: '*Le Printemps adorable a perdu son odeur!*' ('Spring, the Beloved, has lost its scent').[73]

71. I, 192.
72. Proust, op. cit., vol. 8: *Le temps retrouvé*, Paris, 1927, vol. 2, pp. 82ff.
73. I, 89.

In this line Baudelaire expresses something extreme with extreme discretion; this makes it unmistakably his. The word *'perdu'* acknowledges the present state of collapse of that experience which he once shared. The scent is the inaccessible refuge of the *mémoire involontaire*. It is unlikely that it will associate itself with a visual image; of all sensual impressions it will ally itself only with the same scent. If the recognition of a scent is more privileged to provide consolation than any other recollection, this may be so because it deeply drugs the sense of time. A scent may drown years in the odour it recalls. This gives a sense of measureless desolation to Baudelaire's verse. For someone who is past experiencing, there is no consolation. Yet it is this very inability to experience that lies at the heart of rage. An angry man 'won't listen'; his prototype Timon rages against people indiscriminately; he is no longer capable of telling his proven friend from his mortal enemy. D'Aurevilly very perceptively recognized this condition in Baudelaire, calling him 'a Timon with the genius of Archilochus'.[74] The outbreaks of rage are timed to the ticking of the seconds to which the melancholy man is slave.

> Et le Temps m'engloutit minute par minute,
> Comme la neige immense un corps pris de roideur.[75]

> (And, minute by minute, Time engulfs me,
> As the snow's measureless fall covers a motionless body.)

These verses follow immediately after those quoted above. In the *spleen*, time becomes palpable; the minutes cover a man like snow-flakes. This time is outside history, as is that of the *mémoire involontaire*. But in the *spleen* the perception of time is supernaturally keen; every second finds consciousness ready to intercept its shock.[76]

---

74. Barbey d'Aurevilly, *Le XIXe siècle. Les oeuvres et les hommes*, First series, Third part: 'Les poètes', Paris, 1862, p. 381.

75. I, 89.

76. In the mystical 'Colloquy of Monos and Una', Poe has, so to speak, inserted the empty time sequence, to which the man in the mood of 'spleen' is abandoned, into the *durée*, and he seems to regard it as bliss that he is now rid of its horrors. It is a 'sixth sense' acquired by the departed which takes the form of an ability to derive harmony even from the empty passage of time.

Even though chronology places regularity above permanence, it cannot prevent heterogeneous, conspicuous fragments from remaining within it. To have combined recognition of a quality with the measurement of the quantity was the work of the calendars in which the places of recollection are left blank, as it were, in the form of holidays. The man who loses his capacity for experiencing feels as though he is dropped from the calendar. The big-city dweller knows this feeling on Sundays; Baudelaire has it *avant la lettre* in one of the *Spleen* poems.

> Des cloches tout à coup sautent avec furie
> Et lancent vers le ciel un affreux hurlement,
> Ainsi que des esprits errants et sans patrie
> Qui se mettent à geindre opiniâtrement.[77]

> (Suddenly bells leap forth with fury,
> Hurling a hideous howling to the sky
> Like wandering homeless spirits
> Who break into stubborn wailing.)

The bells, which once were part of holidays, have been dropped from the calendar, like the human beings. They are like the poor souls that wander restlessly, but outside of history. If Baudelaire in 'Spleen' and 'Vie antérieure' holds in his hands the scattered fragments of genuine historical experience, Bergson in his conception of the *durée* has become far more estranged from history. 'Bergson the metaphysician suppresses death.'[78] The fact that death is eliminated from Bergson's *durée* isolates it effectively from a his-

To be sure, it is quite easily disrupted by the rhythm of the second-hand. 'There seemed to have sprung up in the brain that of which no words could convey to the merely human intelligence even an indistinct conception. Let me term it a mental pendulous pulsation. It was the moral embodiment of man's abstract idea of *Time*. By the absolute equalization of this movement – or of such as this – had the cycles of the firmamental orbs themselves been adjusted. By its aid I measured the irregularities of the clock upon the mantel, and of the watches of the attendants. Their tickings came sonorously to my ears. The slightest deviation from the true proportion . . . affected me just as violations of abstract truth are wont, on earth, to affect the moral sense.'

77. I, 88.
78. Max Horkheimer, 'Zu Bergsons Metaphysik', in *Zeitschrift für Sozialforschung*, no. 3 (1934), p. 332.

torical (as well as prehistorical) order. Bergson's concept of *action* is in keeping with this. The 'sound common sense' which distinguishes the 'practical man' has been its godfather.[79] The *durée* from which death has been eliminated has the miserable endlessness of a scroll. Tradition is excluded from it.[80] It is the quintessence of a passing moment [*Erlebnis*] that struts about in the borrowed garb of experience. The *spleen*, on the other hand, exposes the passing moment in all its nakedness. To his horror, the melancholy man sees the earth revert to a mere state of nature. No breath of prehistory surrounds it; there is no aura. This is how the earth emerges in the verses of 'Le Goût du néant' which follow the ones we have quoted.

> Je contemple d'en haut le globe en sa rondeur,
> Et je n'y cherche plus l'abri d'une cahute.[81]

> (And from on high I contemplate the globe in its roundness;
> No longer do I look there for the shelter of a hut.)

XI

If we designate as aura the associations which, at home in the *mémoire involontaire*, tend to cluster around the object of a perception, then its analogue in the case of a utilitarian object is the experience which has left traces of the practised hand. The techniques based on the use of the camera and of subsequent analogous mechanical devices extend the range of the *mémoire volontaire*; by means of these devices they make it possible for an event at any time to be permanently recorded in terms of sound and sight. Thus they represent important achievements of a society in which practice

79. cf. Henri Bergson, *Matière et mémoire. Essai sur la relation du corps à l'esprit*, Paris, 1933, pp. 166ff.

80. The deterioration of experience manifests itself in Proust in the complete realization of his ultimate intention. There is nothing more ingenious or more loyal than the way in which he nonchalantly and constantly strives to tell the reader: Redemption is my private show.

81. I, 89.

is in decline. To Baudelaire there was something profoundly un-
nerving and terrifying about daguerreotype; he speaks of the
fascination it exerted as 'startling and cruel'.[82] Thus he must have
sensed, though he certainly did not see through them, the connections of which we have spoken. His willingness always to grant the
modern its place and, especially in art, to assign it its specific function also determined his attitude towards photography. Whenever
he felt it as a threat, he tried to put it down to its 'mistaken developments';[83] yet he admitted that these were promoted by 'the stupidity
of the broad masses'. 'These masses demanded an ideal that would
conform to their aspirations and the nature of their temperament.
. . . Their prayers were granted by a vengeful god, and Daguerre
became his prophet.'[84] Nevertheless, Baudelaire tried to take a
more conciliatory view. Photography should be free to stake out
a claim for ephemeral things, those that have a right 'to a place in
the archives of our memory', as long as it stops short of the 'region
of the intangible, imaginative':[85] that of art in which only that is
allotted a place 'on which man has bestowed the imprint of his soul'.
This is scarcely a Solomon-like judgment. The perpetual readiness
of volitional, discursive memory, encouraged by the technique of
mechanical reproduction, reduces the scope for the play of the
imagination. The latter may perhaps be defined as an ability to give
expression to desires of a special kind, with 'something beautiful'
thought of as their fulfilment. Valéry has set forth the conditions for
this fulfilment: 'We recognize a work of art by the fact that no idea
it inspires in us, no mode of behaviour that it suggests we adopt
could exhaust it or dispose of it. We may inhale the smell of a
flower whose fragrance is agreeable to us for as long as we like;
it is impossible for us to rid ourselves of the fragrance by which
our senses have been aroused, and no recollection, no thought, no
mode of behaviour can obliterate its effect or release us from the
hold it has on us. He who has set himself the task of creating a work
of art aims at the same effect.'[86] According to this view, the painting
we look at reflects back at us that of which our eyes will never have

82. II, 197.   83. II, 224.   84. II, 222ff.
85. II, 224.
86. Valéry, *Avant-propos. Encyclopédie française*, vol. 16: *Arts et littératures dans la société contemporaine*, 1, Paris, 1935, fasc. 16.04–5ff.

their fill. What it contains that fulfils the original desire would be the very same stuff on which the desire continuously feeds. What distinguishes photography from painting is therefore clear, and why there can be no encompassing principle of 'creation' applicable to both: to the eyes that will never have their fill of a painting, photography is rather like food for the hungry or drink for the thirsty.

The crisis of artistic reproduction which manifests itself in this way can be seen as an integral part of a crisis in perception itself. What prevents our delight in the beautiful from ever being satisfied is the image of the past, which Baudelaire regards as veiled by the tears of nostalgia. '*Ach, du warst in abgelebten Zeiten meine Schwester oder meine Frau!*' ('Oh, you were in times gone by my sister or my wife' – Goethe); this declaration of love is the tribute which the beautiful as such is entitled to claim. In so far as art aims at the beautiful and, on however modest a scale, 'reproduces' it, it conjures it up (as Faust does Helen) out of the womb of time.[87] This no longer happens in the case of technical reproduction. (The beautiful has no place in it.) Proust, complaining of the barrenness and lack of depth in the images of Venice that his *mémoire volontaire* presented to him, notes that the very word 'Venice' made that wealth of images seem to him as vapid as an exhibiton of photographs.[88] If the distinctive feature of the images that rise from the *mémoire involontaire* is seen in their aura, then photography is decisively implicated in the phenomenon of the 'decline of the aura'. What was inevitably felt to be inhuman, one might even say deadly, in daguerreotypy was the (prolonged) looking into the camera, since the camera records our likeness without returning our gaze. But looking at someone carries the implicit expectation that our look will be returned by the object of our gaze. Where this expectation is met (which, in the case of thought processes, can apply equally to the look of the eye of the mind and to a glance pure and simple), there is an experience of the aura to the fullest extent.

87. The moment of such a success is itself marked as something unique. It is the basis of the structural design of Proust's works. Each situation in which the chronicler is touched by the breath of lost time is thereby rendered incomparable and removed from the sequence of the days.

88. cf. Proust, op. cit., vol. 8: *Le temps retrouvé*, p. 236.

'Perceptibility,' as Novalis puts it, 'is a kind of attentiveness.'[89] The perceptibility he has in mind is none other than that of the aura. Experience of the aura thus rests on the transposition of a response common in human relationships to the relationship between the inanimate or natural object and man. The person we look at, or who feels he is being looked at, looks at us in turn. To perceive the aura of an object we look at means to invest it with the ability to look at us in return.[90] This experience corresponds to the data of the *mémoire involontaire*. (These data, incidentally, are unique; they are lost to the memory that seeks to retain them. Thus they lend support to a concept of the aura that comprises the 'unique manifestation of a distance'.[91] This designation has the advantage of clarifying the ceremonial character of the phenomenon. The essentially distant is the inapproachable: inapproachability is in fact a primary quality of the ceremonial image.) Proust's great familiarity with the problem of the aura requires no emphasis. Nevertheless, it is notable that he alludes to it at times in terms which comprehend its theory: 'Some people who are fond of secrets flatter themselves that objects retain something of the gaze that has rested on them.' (The ability, it would seem, of returning the gaze.) 'They believe that monuments and pictures present themselves only beneath the delicate veil which centuries of love and reverence on the part of so many admirers have woven about them. This chimera,' Proust concludes evasively, 'would change into truth if they related it to the only reality that is valid for the individual, namely, the world of his emotions.'[92] Valéry's characterization of perception in dreams as aural is akin to this and, by

89. Novalis, *Schriften*, edited by Heilborn, Berlin, 1901, Second part, p. 293.

90. This endowment is a wellspring of poetry. Wherever a human being, an animal, or an inanimate object thus endowed by the poet lifts up its eyes, it draws him into the distance. The gaze of nature thus awakened dreams and pulls the poet after its dream. Words, too, can have an aura of their own. This is how Karl Kraus described it: 'The closer the look one takes at a word, the greater the distance from which it looks back' (Karl Kraus, *Pro domo et mundo*, Munich, 1912, p. 164).

91. Walter Benjamin, 'Das Kunstwerk im Zeitalter seiner technischen Reproduzierbarkeit', in *Zeitschrift für Sozialforschung*, no. 5 (1936), p. 43.

92. Proust, op. cit., vol. 8: *Le temps retrouvé*, Paris, 1927, p. 33.

virtue of its objective orientation, reaches further. 'To say, "Here I see such and such an object" does not establish an equation between me and the object. . . . In dreams, however, there is an equation. The things I see, see me just as much as I see them.'[93] On a level with perception in dreams is the nature of temples, of which Baudelaire said:

> L'homme y passe à travers des forêts de symboles
> Qui l'observent avec des regards familiers.

> (Man wends his way through forests of symbols
> Which look at him with their familiar glances.)

The greater Baudelaire's insight into this phenomenon, the more unmistakably did the disintegration of the aura make itself felt in his lyrical poetry. This occurs in the form of a symbol which we encounter in the *Fleurs du mal* almost invariably whenever the look of the human eye is invoked. (That Baudelaire did not follow some preconceived scheme goes without saying.) What is involved here is that the expectation roused by the look of the human eye is not fulfilled. Baudelaire describes eyes of which one is inclined to say that they have lost their ability to look. Yet this lends them a charm which to a large, perhaps predominant, extent serves as a means of defraying the cost of his instinctual desires. It was under the spell of these eyes that *sexus* in Baudelaire detached itself from *eros*. If in 'Selige Sehnsucht' the lines

> Keine Ferne macht dich schwierig,
> Kommst geflogen und gebannt

> (No distance makes you hesitate; you come flying,
> and stay under a spell [Goethe])

must be regarded as the classic description of that love which is sated with the experience of the aura, then lyric poetry could hardly offer a greater challenge to those lines than Baudelaire's

> Je t'adore à l'égal de la voûte nocturne,
> O vase de tristesse, ô grande taciturne,
> Et t'aime d'autant plus, belle, que tu me fuis,
> Et que tu me parais, ornement de mes nuits,

93. Valéry, *Analecta*, Paris, 1935, pp. 193ff.

> Plus ironiquement accumuler les lieues
> Qui séparent mes bras des immensités bleues.[94]

> (No less than the night's vault do I adore you,
> Vessel of sorrow, O deeply silent one,
> And even more I love you, my lovely one,
> Because you flee from me and, ornament of my nights,
> Ironically you seem to multiply the miles
> That separate my arms from blue immensities.)

The deeper the remoteness which a glance has to overcome, the stronger will be the spell that is apt to emanate from the gaze. In eyes that look at us with a mirrorlike blankness the remoteness remains complete. It is precisely for this reason that such eyes know nothing of distance. Baudelaire incorporated the smoothness of their stare in a subtle couplet:

> Plonge tes yeux dans des yeux fixes
> Des Satyresses ou des Nixes.[95]

> (Let your eyes look deeply into the fixed stare
> Of Satyresses or of Nymphs.)

Female satyrs and nymphs are no longer members of the family of man. Theirs is a world apart. Significantly, Baudelaire injected into his poem the look of the eye encumbered by distance as *regard familier*.[96] The poet who failed to found a family endowed the word *familier* with overtones pervaded by promise and renunciation. He has lost himself to the spell of eyes which do not return his glance and submits to their sway without illusions.

> Tes yeux, illuminés ainsi que des boutiques
> Et des ifs flamboyants dans les fêtes publiques,
> Usent insolemment d'un pouvoir emprunté.[97]

> (Your eyes, lit up like shop windows
> And trees illuminated for public celebrations,
> With insolence make use of borrowed power.)

'Dullness,' says Baudelaire in one of his earliest publications, 'is frequently an ornament of beauty. It is to this that we owe it if eyes

94. I, 40.   95. I, 90.   96. cf. I, 23.   97. I, 40.

are sad and translucent like blackish swamps or if their gaze has the oily inertness of tropical seas.'[98] When such eyes come alive, it is with the self-protective wariness of a wild animal hunting for prey. (Thus the eye of the prostitute scrutinizing the passers-by is at the same time on its guard against the police. Baudelaire found the physiognomic type bred by this kind of life delineated in Constantin Guys's numerous drawings of prostitutes. 'Her eyes, like those of a wild animal, are fixed on the distant horizon; they have the restlessness of a wild animal ... but sometimes also the animal's sudden tense vigilance.'[99]) That the eye of the city dweller is over-burdened with protective functions is obvious. Georg Simmel refers to some less obvious tasks with which it is charged. 'The person who is able to see but unable to hear is much more ... troubled than the person who is able to hear but unable to see. Here is something . . . characteristic of the big city. The interpersonal relationships of people in big cities are characterized by a markedly greater emphasis on the use of the eyes than on that of the ears. This can be attributed chiefly to the institution of public convey-ances. Before buses, railroads, and trams became fully established during the nineteenth century, people were never put in a position of having to stare at one another for minutes or even hours on end without exchanging a word.'[100]

There is no daydreaming surrender to faraway things in the pro-tective eye. It may even cause one to feel something like pleasure in the degradation of such abandonment. This is probably the sense in which the following curious sentences should be read. In his 'Salon de 1859' Baudelaire lets the landscapes pass in review, concluding with this admission: 'I long for the return of the dioramas whose enormous, crude magic subjects me to the spell of a useful illusion. I prefer looking at the backdrop paintings of the stage where I find my favourite dreams treated with consummate skill and tragic concision. Those things, so completely false, are for that very reason much closer to the truth, whereas the majority of our land-scape painters are liars, precisely because they fail to lie.'[101] One is

98. II, 622.   99. II, 359.
100. Georg Simmel, *Mélanges de philosophie rélativiste*, translated by A. Guillain, Paris, 1912, pp. 26ff.
101. II, 273.

inclined to attach less importance to the 'useful illusion' than to the *tragic* concision'. Baudelaire insists on the magic of distance; he goes so far as to judge landscapes by the standard of paintings in the booths at fairs. Does he mean the magic of distance to be pierced, as must needs happen when the spectator steps too close to the depicted scene? This is embodied in one of the great verses of the *Fleurs du mal*:

> Le Plaisir vaporeux fuira vers l'horizon
> Ainsi qu'une sylphide au fond de la coulisse.[102]

> (Nebulous Pleasure horizonward will flee,
> Just like a sylph behind the wings.)

XII

Les Fleurs du mal was the last lyric work that had a European repercussion; no later work penetrated beyond a more or less limited linguistic area. Added to this is the fact that Baudelaire expended his productive capacity almost entirely on this one work. And, finally, it cannot be denied that some of his motifs – and the present study has dealt with them – render the possibility of lyric poetry questionable. These three facts define Baudelaire historically. They show that he imperturbably stuck to his cause and single-mindedly concentrated on his mission. He went so far as to proclaim as his goal 'the creation of a cliché'.[103] In this he saw the condition of every future poet; he had a low opinion of those who were not up to it. 'Do you drink beef tea made of ambrosia? Do you eat cutlets from Paros? How much do they give in the pawn-shop for a lyre?'[104] To Baudelaire, the lyric poet with a halo is antiquated. In a prose piece which came to light at a late date, 'A Lost Halo', Baudelaire has such a poet appear as a supernumerary. When Baudelaire's literary remains were first examined, this piece

102. I, 94.
103. cf. Jules Lemaître, *Les contemporains. Etudes et portraits littéraires*, Paris, 1895, p. 29 and Paris, 1886, p. 133.
104. II, 422.

was rejected as 'unsuitable for publication'; to this day it has been neglected by Baudelaire scholarship.

' "What do I see, my dear fellow? *You – here?* I find *you* in a place of ill repute – a man who sips quintessences, who consumes ambrosia? Really! I couldn't be more surprised."

' "You know, my dear fellow, how afraid I am of horses and carriages. A short while ago I was hurrying across the boulevard, and midst this moving chaos in which death comes galloping at you from all sides at once I must have made an awkward movement, for the halo slipped off my head and fell onto the muddy asphalt pavement. I didn't have the courage to pick it up, and decided that it hurts less to lose one's insignia than to have one's bones broken. And furthermore, I said to myself, every cloud has a silver lining. Now I can go about incognito, do bad things, and indulge in vulgar behaviour like ordinary mortals. So here I am, just like you!"

' "But you ought to report the loss of your halo or inquire at the lost property office."

' "I wouldn't dream of it. I like it here. You are the only person who has recognized me. Besides, dignity bores me. And I enjoy the thought that some bad poet will pick up the halo and won't think twice about adorning himself with it. There is nothing I like better than to make someone happy – especially if the happy man is one I can laugh at. Just picture X. wearing it, or Y.! Won't that be funny?" '[105]

The same motif may be found in the diaries; only the ending is different. The poet quickly picks the halo up; but now he is bothered by the feeling that the incident may be a bad omen.[106, 107]

The man who wrote these pieces was no *flâneur*. They embody, in ironic form, the same experiences which Baudelaire put into this sentence, without any trimmings and in passing: '*Perdu dans ce vilain monde*, coudoyé par les foules, *je suis comme un homme lassé dont l'oeil ne voit en arrière, dans les années profondes, que désabusement et amertume, et, devant lui, qu'un orage où rien de neuf n'est contenu, ni enseignement ni douleur*'[108] ('Lost in this mean world,

105. I, 483ff.   106. cf. II, 634.

107. It is not impossible that this entry was occasioned by a pathogenic shock. The form which relates it to Baudelaire's work is all the more revealing.

108. II, 641 [Benjamin's emphasis].

jostled by the crowd, I am like a weary man whose eye, looking backwards, into the depth of the years, sees nothing but disillusion and bitterness, and before him nothing but a tempest which contains nothing new, neither instruction nor pain.') Of all the experiences which made his life what it was, Baudelaire singled out his having been jostled by the crowd as the decisive, unique experience. The lustre of a crowd with a motion and a soul of its own, the glitter that had bedazzled the *flâneur*, had dimmed for him. To impress the crowd's meanness upon himself, he envisaged the day on which even the lost women, the outcasts, would be ready to advocate a well-ordered life, condemn libertinism, and reject everything except money. Having been betrayed by these last allies of his, Baudelaire battled the crowd – with the impotent rage of someone fighting the rain or the wind. This is the nature of something lived through (*Erlebnis*) to which Baudelaire has given the weight of an experience (*Erfahrung*). He indicated the price for which the sensation of the modern age may be had: the disintegration of the aura in the experience of shock. He paid dearly for consenting to this disintegration – but it is the law of his poetry, which shines in the sky of the Second Empire as 'a star without atmosphere'.[109]

109. Friedrich Nietzsche, *Unzeitgemässe Betrachtungen*, Leipzig, 1893, p. 164.

Paris – the Capital of the Nineteenth Century

Translated from the German by Quintin Hoare

The waters are blue and the plants are pink; the evening is sweet to look upon; one goes for a stroll. The great ladies are out for a stroll; behind them play the little ladies.

Nguyen Trong Hiep, *Paris, Capital of France* (1897)

I. Fourier or the Arcades

De ces palais les colonnes magiques
A l'amateur montrent de toutes parts
Dans les objets qu'étalent leurs portiques
Que l'industrie est rivale des arts.

('The magic columns of these palaces show to the amateur on every side, in the articles which their porticos display, that industry rivals the arts.')

Nouveaux tableaux de Paris (1828)

Most of the Paris arcades came into being during the decade and a half which followed 1822. The first condition of their emergence was the boom in the textile trade. The *magasins de nouveauté*, the first establishments that kept large stocks of goods on the premises, began to appear. They were the forerunners of the department stores. It was the time of which Balzac wrote: 'The great poem of display chants its stanzas of colour from the Madeleine to the gate of Saint-Denis' ('*Le grand poème de l'étalage chant ses*

strophes de couleur depuis la Madeleine jusqu'à la porte Saint-Denis').
The arcades were centres of the luxury-goods trade. The manner
in which they were fitted out displayed Art in the service of the
salesman. Contemporaries never tired of admiring them. For long
afterwards they remained a point of attraction for foreigners. An
illustrated Paris guide said: 'These arcades, a new contrivance of
industrial luxury, are glass-covered, marble-floored passages
through entire blocks of houses, whose proprietors have joined
forces in the venture. On both sides of these passages, which obtain
their light from above, there are arrayed the most elegant shops,
so that such an arcade is a city, indeed a world, in miniature.' The
arcades were the setting for the first gas-lighting.

The beginnings of construction in iron constituted the second
condition for the appearance of the arcades. The Empire had seen
in this technique a contribution to the renewal of architecture in the
sense of ancient Greece. The architectural theorist Bötticher expressed the general conviction when he said that 'with regard to the
art-forms of the new system, the formal principle of the Hellenic
mode' must come into force. Empire was the style of revolutionary
terrorism, for which the State was an end in itself. Just as Napoleon
little realized the functional nature of the State as instrument of the
rule of the bourgeois class, so the master-builders of his time equally
little realized the functional nature of iron, with which the con-
structional principle entered upon its rule in architecture. These
master-builders fashioned supports in the style of the Pompeian
column, factories in the style of dwelling-houses, just as later the
first railway stations were modelled on *chalets*. 'Construction
occupies the role of the subconscious.' Nevertheless, the concept
of the engineer, which came originally from the Revolutionary
Wars, began to gain ground, and the struggles between builder and
decorator, Ecole Polytechnique and Ecole des Beaux Arts, began.

With iron, an artificial building material appeared for the first
time in the history of architecture. It went through a development
whose tempo accelerated during the course of the century. This
received its decisive impulse when it turned out that the locomotive
with which experiments had been made since the end of the twenties
could only be utilized on iron rails. The rail was the first iron unit
of construction, the forerunner of the girder. Iron was avoided for

dwelling-houses, and made use of for arcades, exhibition halls, railway stations – buildings which served transitory purposes. Simultaneously, the architectonic areas in which glass was employed were extended. But the social conditions for its increased utilization as a building material only came into being a hundred years later. In Scheerbart's *Glass Architecture* (1914) it still appeared in the context of the Utopia.

Chaque époque rêve la suivante.

('Every epoch dreams its successor.')

Michelet, *Avenir! Avenir!*

To the form of the new means of production, which to begin with is still dominated by the old (Marx), there correspond images in the collective consciousness in which the new and the old are inter-mingled. These images are ideals, and in them the collective seeks not only to transfigure, but also to transcend, the immaturity of the social product and the deficiencies of the social order of production. In these ideals there also emerges a vigorous aspiration to break with what is out-dated – which means, however, with the most recent past. These tendencies turn the fantasy, which gains its initial stimulus from the new, back upon the primal past. In the dream in which every epoch sees in images the epoch which is to succeed it, the latter appears coupled with elements of prehistory – that is to say of a classless society. The experiences of this society, which have their store-place in the collective unconscious, interact with the new to give birth to the utopias which leave their traces in a thousand configurations of life, from permanent buildings to ephemeral fashions.

These relationships became discernible in the Utopia devised by Fourier. Their innermost origin lay in the appearance of machines. But this fact was not expressed directly in their utopian presenta-tion; this derived both from the amorality of the market society and from the false morality mustered to serve it. The phalanstery was to lead men back into relations in which morality would become superfluous. Its highly complicated organization resembled machinery. The imbrications of the *passions*, the intricate combination of the *passions mécanistes* with the *passion cabaliste*, were primitive analogies based on the machine, formed in the material of psychology. This machinery, formed of men, produced the land of Cockaigne, the primal wish-symbol, that Fourier's Utopia had filled with new life.

In the arcades, Fourier had seen the architectonic canon for the phalanstery. Their reactionary transformation at Fourier's hands was characteristic: while they originally served social ends, with him they became dwelling-places. The phalanstery became a city of arcades. Fourier established in the narrow formal world of the Empire the highly-coloured idyll of Biedermeier. Its fading brilliance lasted until Zola. The latter took over Fourier's ideas in his *Travail*, just as he took his leave of the arcades in *Thérèse Raquin*.

Marx took up the cudgels on Fourier's behalf, defending him from Carl Grün, and stressed his 'gargantuan concept of man'. He also turned his attention to Fourier's humour. As a matter of fact, Jean Paul in his *Levana* is as related to Fourier the pedagogue as Scheerbart in his *Glass Architecture* is to Fourier the creator of Utopias.

II. Daguerre or the Dioramas

Soleil, prends garde à toi!

('Sun, look out for yourself!')

A. J. Wiertz, *Oeuvres littéraires* (Paris, 1870)

With construction in iron, architecture began to outgrow art; painting did the same in its turn with the dioramas. Preparation for the dioramas reached its peak just at the moment when the arcades began to appear. Tireless efforts had been made to render the dioramas, by means of technical artifice, the *locus* of a perfect imitation of nature. People sought to copy the changing time of day in the countryside, the rising of the moon, or the rushing of the waterfall. David counselled his pupils to draw from Nature in their dioramas. While the dioramas strove to produce life-like transformations in the Nature portrayed in them, they foreshadowed, via photography, the moving-picture and the talking-picture.

Contemporary with the dioramas there was a dioramic literature. *Le Livre des cent-et-un*, *Les Français peints par eux-mêmes*, *Le Diable à Paris*, *La Grande ville* belonged to this. These books were a preparation for the belletristic collective work for which Girardin created a home in the thirties with the *feuilleton*. They consisted of individual sketches whose anecdotal form corresponded to the plastically arranged foreground of the dioramas, and whose documentary content corresponded to their painted background. This literature was socially dioramic too. For the last time the worker appeared, away from his class, as a stage-extra in an idyll.

The dioramas, which signalled a revolution in the relationship of art to technology, were at the same time the expression of a new attitude to life. The town-dweller, whose political supremacy over the countryside was frequently expressed in the course of the century, made an attempt to bring the country into the town. In the dioramas, the town was transformed into landscape, just as it was later in a subtler way for the *flâneurs*. Daguerre was a pupil of the diorama-painter Prévost, whose establishment was situated in the Arcade of the Dioramas. Description of the dioramas of Prévost and of Daguerre. In 1839 Daguerre's diorama was burned down. In the same year he announced the invention of the daguerreotype.

Arago presented photography in a speech in the Assembly. He assigned to it its place in the history of technical science. He prophesied its scientific applications. Whereupon the artists began to debate its artistic value. Photography led to the destruction of the great profession of the miniature-portraitists. This did not happen purely for economic reasons. The early photography was artistically superior to miniature-portraiture. The technical reason for this lay in the long exposure time, which necessitated the most intense concentration on the part of the subject. The social reason for it lay in the circumstance that the first photographers belonged to the *avant-garde* and that their clientele for the most part came from it. Nadar's lead over his professional colleagues was demonstrated when he embarked on taking pictures in the Paris sewers. Thus for the first time discoveries were required of the lens. And its significance became all the greater as, in the light of the new technical and social reality, the subjective contribution to painted and graphic information was seen to be increasingly questionable.

The World Exhibition of 1855 was the first to have a special exhibit called 'Photography'. In the same year Wiertz published his great article on photography, in which he assigned to it the philosophical enlightenment of painting. He understood this enlightenment, as his own paintings show, in a political sense. Wiertz can thus be designated as the first person who, although he did not foresee, at least demanded montage, as the agitational utilization of photography. As the technique of communications increased, the informational importance of painting diminished. The latter began, in reaction to photography, first to emphasize the coloured elements of the image. As Impressionism gave way to Cubism, painting created for itself a broader domain, into which for the time being photography could not follow it. Photography in its turn, from the middle of the century onwards, extended enormously the sphere of the market-society; for it offered on the market, in limitless quantities, figures, landscapes, events which had previously been utilizable either not at all, or only as pictures for one customer. And in order to increase sales, it renewed its objects by means of modish variations in camera-technique, which determined the subsequent history of photography.

III. Grandville or the World Exhibitions

Oui, quand le monde entier, de Paris jusqu'en Chine,
O divin Saint-Simon, sera dans ta doctrine,
L'âge d'or doit renaître avec tout son éclat,
Les fleuves rouleront du thé, du chocolat;
Les moutons tout rôtis bondiront dans la plaine,
Et les brochets au bleu nageront dans la Seine;
Les épinards viendront au monde fricassés,
Avec des croûtons frits tout au tour concassés.
Les arbres produiront des pommes en compotes
Et l'on moissonnera des cerricks et des bottes;
Il neigera du vin, il pleuvera des poulets,
Et du ciel les canards tomberont aux navets.

('Yes, when the entire world, from Paris as far as China,
O divine Saint-Simon, follows your doctrine, then must
the Golden Age return in all its brilliance, the rivers will
flow with tea, with chocolate; sheep already roasted will
gambol in the plain, and buttered pike will swim in the
Seine; cooked spinach will spring from the ground,
with a border of *croûtons*. The trees will bear stewed
apples, and bales and sheaves will be harvested; wine will
fall like snow, and chickens like rain, and ducks will drop
from the sky with a garnish of turnips.')

Lauglé et Vanderbusch, *Louis et le Saint-Simonien*
(1832)

World exhibitions were places of pilgrimage to the fetish Commodity. 'All Europe has set off to view goods' (*'L'Europe s'est déplacé pour voir des marchandises'*), said Taine in 1855. The world exhibitions were preceded by national exhibitions of industry, of which the first took place in 1798 on the Champs de Mars. This was a result of the desire 'to amuse the working class, and becomes for them a festival of emancipation'. The workers were to the fore as customers. The framework of the entertainment industry had not yet been formed. The public festival provided it. Chaptal's speech on industry opened this exhibition.

The Saint-Simonians, who projected the industrialization of the earth, take up the idea of world exhibitions. Chevalier, the first authority in the new field, was a pupil of Enfantin and editor of the Saint-Simonian paper *Globe*. The Saint-Simonians had anticipated the development of the world economy, but not the class struggle. Their part in industrial and commercial enterprises around the middle of the century went together with a helplessness in those questions which concerned the proletariat. The world exhibitions glorified the exchange-value of commodities. They created a framework in which their use-value receded into the background. They poened up a phantasmagoria into which people entered in order to be distracted. The entertainment industry made that easier for them by lifting them to the level of the commodity. They yielded to its manipulations while enjoying their alienation from themselves and from others.

The enthronement of the commodity and the glitter of distraction around it was the secret theme of Grandville's art. The correlative to this was the ambivalence between its utopian and its cynical element. Its refinements in the representation of dead objects corresponded to what Marx calls the 'theological capers' of the commodity. They took clear shape in the *spécialité*: under Grandville's pencil, a way of designating goods which came into use around this time in the luxury industry, transformed the whole of Nature into specialities. He presented the latter in the same spirit in which advertisements – this word too (*réclames*) came into existence at that time – were beginning to present their wares. He ended in madness.

Fashion: Mr Death! Mr Death!

Leopardi, *Dialogue between Fashion and Death*

The world exhibitions erected the universe of commodities. Grand-ville's fantasies transmitted commodity-character onto the universe. They modernized it. The ring of Saturn became a cast-iron balcony, upon which the inhabitants of Saturn take the air of an evening. The literary counterpart of this graphic Utopia was represented by the books of Fourier's follower, the naturalist Toussenel.

Fashion prescribed the ritual by which the fetish Commodity wished to be worshipped, and Grandville extended the sway of fashion over the objects of daily use as much as over the cosmos. In pursuing it to its extremes, he revealed its nature. It stands in opposition to the organic. It prostitutes the living body to the inorganic world. In relation to the living it represents the rights of the corpse. Fetishism, which succumbs to the sex-appeal of the inorganic, is its vital nerve; and the cult of the commodity recruits this to its service.

Victor Hugo published a manifesto for the Paris World Exhibition of 1867: 'To the Peoples of Europe'. Their interests had been championed earlier and more unequivocally by the delegations of French workers, of which the first had been sent to the London World Exhibition of 1851, and the second, of 750 members, to that of 1862. The latter was of direct importance for Marx's foundation of the International Workingmen's Association.

The phantasmagoria of capitalist culture attained its most radiant unfurling in the World Exhibition of 1867. The Second Empire was at the height of its power. Paris was confirmed in its position as the capital of luxury and of fashion. Offenbach set the rhythm for Parisian life. The operetta was the ironical Utopia of a lasting domination by Capital.

IV. Louis-Philippe or the Interior

La tête . . . sur la table de nuit, comme une renoncule,
Repose.

('The head . . . rests upon the night-table like a ranunculus.')

Baudelaire, 'Une Martyre'

Under Louis-Philippe, the private citizen entered upon the historical scene. The extension of the apparatus of democracy by means of a new electoral law coincided with the parliamentary corruption that was organized by Guizot. Under cover of this, the ruling class made history while it pursued its business affairs. It encouraged the construction of railways in order to improve its holdings. It supported the rule of Louis-Philippe as that of the managing director. With the July Revolution the bourgeoisie had realized the aims of 1789 (Marx).

For the private citizen, for the first time the living-space became distinguished from the place of work. The former constituted itself as the interior. The office was its complement. The private citizen who in the office took reality into account, required of the interior that it should support him in his illusions. This necessity was all the more pressing since he had no intention of adding social preoccupations to his business ones. In the creation of his private environment he suppressed them both. From this sprang the phantasmagorias of the interior. This represented the universe for the private citizen. In it he assembled the distant in space and in time. His drawing-room was a box in the world-theatre.

Statement on *art nouveau*. The shattering of the interior took place around the turn of the century in *art nouveau*. And yet the latter appeared, according to its ideology, to bring with it the perfecting of the interior. The transfiguration of the lone soul was its apparent aim. Individualism was its theory. With Van de Velde, there appeared the house as expression of the personality. Ornament was to such a house what the signature is to a painting. The real significance of *art nouveau* was not expressed in this ideology. It represented the last attempt at a sortie on the part of Art imprisoned by technical advance within her ivory tower. It mobilized all the reserve forces of interiority. They found their expression in the mediumistic language of line, in the flower as symbol of the naked, vegetable Nature that confronted the technologically armed environment. The new elements of construction in iron – girder-forms – obsessed *art nouveau*. Through ornament, it strove to win back these forms for Art. Concrete offered it new possibilities for the creation of plastic forms in architecture. Around this time the real centre of gravity of the sphere of existence was displaced to the office. The de-realized centre of gravity created its abode in the private home. Ibsen's *Master Builder* summed up *art nouveau*: the attempt of the individual, on the strength of his interiority, to vie with technical progress leads to his downfall.

Je crois . . . à mon âme: la Chose.

('I believe . . . in my soul: the Thing.')

Léon Deubel, *Oeuvres* (Paris, 1929)

The interior was the place of refuge of Art. The collector was the true inhabitant of the interior. He made the glorification of things his concern. To him fell the task of Sisyphus which consisted of stripping things of their commodity character by means of his possession of them. But he conferred upon them only a fancier's value, rather than use-value. The collector dreamed that he was in a world which was not only far-off in distance and in time, but which was also a better one, in which to be sure people were just as poorly provided with what they needed as in the world of everyday, but in which things were free from the bondage of being useful.

The interior was not only the private citizen's universe, it was also his casing. Living means leaving traces. In the interior, these were stressed. Coverings and antimacassars, boxes and casings, were devised in abundance, in which the traces of everyday objects were moulded. The resident's own traces were also moulded in the interior. The detective story appeared, which investigated these traces. The *Philosophy of Furniture*, as much as his detective stories, shows Poe to have been the first physiognomist of the interior. The criminals of the first detective novels were neither gentlemen nor apaches, but middle-class private citizens.

V. Baudelaire or the Streets of Paris

Tout pour moi devient allégorie.

('Everything, for me, becomes allegory.')

Baudelaire, 'Le Cygne'

Baudelaire's genius, which drew its nourishment from melancholy, was an allegorical one. With Baudelaire, Paris for the first time became the subject of lyrical poetry. This poetry is no local folklore; the allegorist's gaze which falls upon the city is rather the gaze of alienated man. It is the gaze of the *flâneur*, whose way of living still bestowed a conciliatory gleam over the growing destitution of men in the great city. The *flâneur* still stood at the margin, of the great city as of the bourgeois class. Neither of them had yet overwhelmed him. In neither of them was he at home. He sought his asylum in the crowd. Early contributions to the physiognomy of the crowd are to be found in Engels and in Poe. The crowd was the veil from behind which the familiar city as phantasmagoria beckoned to the *flâneur*. In it, the city was now landscape, now a room. And both of these went into the construction of the department store, which made use of *flânerie* itself in order to sell goods. The department store was the *flâneur's* final coup.

As *flâneurs*, the intelligentsia came into the market-place. As they thought, to observe it – but in reality it was already to find a buyer. In this intermediary stage, in which they still had Maecenases, but were already beginning to familiarize themselves with the market, they took the form of the *bohème*. To the uncertainty of their economic position corresponded the uncertainty of their political function. The most spectacular expression of this was provided by the professional conspirators, who without exception belonged to the *bohème*. Their first field of activity was the army, later on it became the petty bourgeoisie, and on occasion the proletariat. However, this group saw in the real leaders of the latter its adversary. The *Communist Manifesto* put an end to its political existence. Baudelaire's poetry drew its force from the rebellious pathos of this group. He took the part of the asocial. He achieved his only sexual relationship with a whore.

Facilis descensus Averni.

('The road to Hell is easy.')

Virgil, *Aeneid*

It is the unique quality of Baudelaire's poetry that the images of Woman and of Death intermingle in a third – that of Paris. The Paris of his poems is a sunken city, and more submarine than subterranean. The chthonic elements of the city – its topographical formation, the old abandoned bed of the Seine – have indeed found in him a mould. Yet with Baudelaire, in the 'death-loving idyll' of the city, there is decidedly a social, and modern, sub-stratum. The modern is a main stress in his poetry. As spleen he shatters the ideal ('Spleen et Idéal'). But it is precisely the modern which always conjures up prehistory. That happens here through the ambiguity which is peculiar to the social relations and events of this epoch. Ambiguity is the figurative appearance of the dialectic, the law of the dialectic at a standstill. This standstill is Utopia, and the dialectical image therefore a dream image. The commodity clearly provides such an image: as fetish. The arcades, which are both house and stars, provide such an image. And such an image is provided by the whore, who is seller and commodity in one.

Le voyage pour connâitre ma géographie.

('The journey to discover my geography.')

Diary of a Madman (Paris, 1907)

The last poem of the *Fleurs du mal*, 'Le Voyage': 'O death, old captain, it is time, let us weigh anchor (*'O mort, vieux capitaine, il est temps! levons l'ancre!'*). The *flâneur*'s last journey: death. Its goal: novelty. 'To the depths of the unknown to find something new' (*'Au fond de l'Inconnu pour trouver du* nouveau!'). Novelty is a quality which does not depend on the use-value of the commodity. It is the source of the illusion which belongs inalienably to the images which the collective unconscious engenders. It is the quintessence of false consciousness, of which fashion is the tireless agent. This illusion of novelty is reflected, like one mirror in another, in the illusion of infinite sameness. The product of this reflection is the phantasmagoria of 'cultural history' in which the bourgeoisie enjoyed its false consciousness to the full. Art, which begins to have doubts about its function, and ceases to be *'inséparable de l'utilité'* (Baudelaire), is forced to make novelty its highest value. Its *arbiter novarum rerum* becomes the snob. He is for art what the dandy is for fashion.

Just as in the seventeenth century allegory becomes the canon of dialectical imagery, so in the nineteenth century does *nouveauté*. And the newspapers march shoulder to shoulder with the *magasins de nouveauté*. The press organizes the market of spiritual values, upon which at first a boom develops. The non-conformists rebel against the surrender of art to the market. They rally round the banner of *l'art pour l'art*. From this slogan there springs the conception of the total work of art, which attempts to isolate art against the development of technology. The rites with which it is celebrated are the counterpart of the distractions which transfigure the commodity. Both abstract from the social being of man. Baudelaire succumbs to the infatuation of Wagner.

VI. Haussmann or the Barricades

J'ai le culte du Beau, du Bien, des grandes choses,
De la belle nature inspirant le grand art,
Qu'il enchante l'oreille ou charme le regard;
J'ai l'amour du printemps en fleurs: femmes et roses.

('I worship the Beautiful, the Good, great things, beautiful nature inspiring great art, whether it enchants the ear or charms the eye; I love the spring in flowers: women and roses.')

Baron Haussmann, *Confession d'un lion devenu vieux*

Das Blüthenreich der Dekorationen,
Der Reiz der Landschaft, der Architektur
Und aller Szenerie-Effekt beruhen
Auf dem Gesetz der Perspektive nur.

('The wealth of decoration, the charm of the countryside, of architecture and of all scenery-effects only depend upon the law of perspective.')

Franz Böhle, *Theater-Katechismus*

Haussmann's urbanistic ideal was one of views in perspective down long street-vistas. It corresponded to the tendency which was noticeable again and again during the nineteenth century, to ennoble technical exigencies with artistic aims. The institutions of the worldly and spiritual rule of the bourgeoisie, set in the frame of the boulevards, were to find their apotheosis. Before their completion, boulevards were covered over with tarpaulins, and unveiled like monuments.

Haussmann's efficiency fitted in well with the idealism of Louis Napoleon. The latter encouraged finance capital. Paris experienced a great speculative boom. Speculation on the stock-exchange pushed into the background the forms of gambling that had come down from feudal society. To the phantasmagoria of space, to which the *flâneur* was addicted, there corresponded the phantasmagoria of time, to which the gambler dedicated himself. Gambling transformed time into a narcotic. Lafargue defined gambling as a miniature reproduction of the mysteries of the market-situation. The expropriations caused by Haussmann engendered a wave of fraudulent speculation. The judgments of the Court of Appeal, which drew its inspiration from the bourgeois and Orleanist opposition, increased the financial risk of Haussmannization. Haussmann attempted to shore up his dictatorship and to place Paris under an emergency régime. In 1864 he expressed his hatred for the rootless population of the great city in a speech in the Assembly. This population kept increasing as a result of his works. The increase of rents drove the proletariat into the outskirts. The Paris *quartiers* thereby lost their characteristic physiognomy. The red belt appeared. Haussmann gave himself the name *artiste démolisseur*. He felt a vocation for his work and stressed the fact in his memoirs. Meanwhile, as far as the Parisians were concerned, he alienated their city from them. They no longer felt at home in it. They began to become conscious of the inhuman character of the great city. Maxime Du Camp's monumental work *Paris* owed its origin to this consciousness. The *Jérémiades d'un Haussmannisé* gave it the form of a biblical lament.

The real aim of Haussmann's works was the securing of the city against civil war. He wished to make the erection of barricades in Paris impossible for all time. With the same purpose, Louis-Philippe had already introduced wooden paving. Nonetheless, the barricades played a role in the February Revolution. Engels gave some thought to the technique of barricade fighting. Haussmann intended to put a stop to it in two ways. The breadth of the streets was to make the erection of barricades impossible, and new streets were to provide the shortest route between the barracks and the working-class areas. Contemporaries christened the undertaking 'strategic beautification' (*L'embellissement stratégique*).

> Fais voir, en déjouant la ruse,
> O République, à ces pervers
> Ta grande face de Méduse
> Au milieu de rouges éclairs.

> ('Reveal, by thwarting their trick,
> O Republic, to those evil men
> your great Medusa's face amidst
> red lightning-flashes.')

> Workers' song around 1850

The barricade was resurrected anew during the Commune. It was stronger and safer than ever. It extended across the great boulevards, often reached first-storey level, and shielded the trenches situated behind it. As the *Communist Manifesto* ended the epoch of the professional conspirators, so the Commune put an end to the phantasmagoria that held sway over the freedom of the proletariat. It shattered the illusion that the task of the proletarian revolution was to complete, hand in hand with the bourgeoisie, the work of 1789. This illusion dominated the period from 1831 to 1871, from the Lyons Uprising to the Commune. The bourgeoisie had never shared this misapprehension. Its struggle against the social rights of the proletariat began right from the great Revolution, and coincided with the philanthropic movement, which masked it and which experienced its most significant development under Napoleon III. Under him, there appeared the movement's monumental work: Le Play's *Ouvriers européens*. Side by side with the concealed position of philanthropy, the bourgeoisie has at all times occupied the open one of the class struggle. As early as in 1831 it recognized in the *Journal des Débats*: 'Every manufacturer lives in his factory like the plantation-owner among his slaves.' The failure of the old working-class insurrections was brought about by the fact that no theory of revolution showed them the way, but on the other hand this was also the condition of the immediate power and enthusiasm with which it set about the construction of a new society. This enthusiasm, which reached its peak in the Commune, at times won over to the working class the best elements of the bourgeoisie, but in the end led it to defeat at the hands of its worst elements. Rimbaud and Courbet declared themselves for the Commune. The burning of Paris was a fitting conclusion to Haussmann's work of destruction.

My good father had been in Paris.

Karl Gutzkow, *Letters from Paris* (1842)

Balzac was the first to speak of the ruins of the bourgeoisie. But it was Surrealism which first allowed its gaze to roam freely over it. The development of the forces of production had turned the wish-symbols of the previous century into rubble, even before the monuments which represented them had crumbled. This development during the nineteenth century liberated the forms of creation from art, just as in the sixteenth century the sciences freed themselves from philosophy. A start is made by architecture as engineering. There followed the reproduction of Nature as photography. The fantasy creations prepare themselves to become practical as commercial art. In the *feuilleton*, poetry submits to the exigencies of montage. All these products are on the point of entering the market as commodities. But they still linger on the threshold. From this epoch spring the arcades and the interiors, the exhibition halls and the dioramas. They are residues of a dream-world. The utilization of dream-elements in waking is the textbook example of dialectical thought. Hence dialectical thought is the organ of historical awakening. Every epoch not only dreams the next, but while dreaming impels it towards wakefulness. It bears its end within itself, and reveals it – as Hegel already recognized – by ruse. With the upheaval of the market economy, we begin to recognize the monuments of the bourgeoisie as ruins even before they have crumbled.

Index

Index